THE AMERICAN KENNEL CLUB'S
Meet the
Boxer™

The Responsible Dog Owner's Handbook

AKC's Meet the Breeds Series

BOWTIE
P R E S S®

Irvine, California
A Division of BowTie, Inc.

AN OFFICIAL PUBLICATION OF THE AMERICAN KENNEL CLUB

AMERICAN
KENNEL CLUB™

Brought to you by The American Kennel Club and The American Boxer Club.
Lead Editor: Lindsay Hanks
Art Director: Cindy Kassebaum
Production Supervisor: Jessica Jaensch
Assistant Production Manager: Tracy Vogtman
Book Project Specialist: Karen Julian

Vice President, Chief Content Officer: June Kikuchi
Vice President, Kennel Club Books: Andrew DePrisco
BowTie Press: Jennifer Calvert, Amy Deputato, Lindsay Hanks, Karen Julian, Jarelle S. Stein

Photographs by: The American Boxer Club (Courtesy of Stephanie Abraham): Cover, 21; Blackhawk Productions (Dwight Dyke): Cover Inset, 4, 9, 34-35, 44, 88, 112-113; BowTie Studio: 32, 37, 39, 42, 50, 65, 124; Diane Lewis Photography: 11, 18-19, 45, 46-47, 62, 67, 69, 70-71, 84-85, 94; Fox Hill Photo (Paulette Johnson): Back Cover, 22, 29, 38, 49, 53, 54, 56, 63, 64, 72, 73, 74, 75, 79, 82, 86, 89, 90, 92-93, 95, 96, 97, 98, 99, 100, 105, 106, 108, 111, 116, 117; Infocus By Miguel (Miguel Betancourt): 15-16; Mark Raycroft: Cover Insets, 1, 3, 4, 6-7, 12, 13, 17, 20, 26, 28, 31, 33, 40, 43, 51, 57, 58, 60-61, 77, 80, 81, 83, 102-103, 114, 115, 118, 119, 121; Shutterstock: 4, 16, 23, 41, 66.

BowTie Press®
Division of BOWTIE INC.
3 Burroughs, Irvine, CA 92618

Library of Congress Cataloging-in-Publication Data

The American Kennel Club's meet the boxer : the responsible dog owner's handbook.
       p. cm. -- (Akc's meet the breeds series)
  Includes bibliographical references and index.
   ISBN 978-1-935484-74-5
 1. Boxer (Dog breed) I. American Kennel Club.
   SF429.B75A47 2011
   636.73--dc23

                          2011042301

Printed and bound in the United States
14 13 12 11 1 2 3 4 5 6 7 8 9 10

Meet Your New Dog

Welcome to *Meet the Boxer*. Whether you're a long-time Boxer owner, or you've just gotten your first puppy, we wish you a lifetime of happiness and enjoyment with your new pet.

In this book, you'll learn about the history of the breed, receive tips on feeding, grooming, and training, and learn about all the fun you can have with your dog. The American Kennel Club and BowTie Press hope that this book serves as a useful guide on the lifelong journey you'll take with your canine companion.

Owned and cherished by millions across America, Boxers make wonderful companions that also enjoy taking part in a variety of dog sports, including Conformation (dog shows), Obedience, Rally®, and Agility.

Thousands of Boxers have also earned the AKC Canine Good Citizen® certification by demonstrating their good manners at home and in the community. We hope that you and your Boxer will become involved in AKC events, too! Learn how to get involved at www.akc.org /events or find a training club in your area at www.akc.org/events/trainingclubs.cfm.

We encourage you to connect with other Boxer owners on the AKC website (www.akc .org), Facebook (www.facebook.com/american kennelclub), and Twitter (@akcdoglovers). Also visit the website for the Boxer Club of America (www.americanboxerclub.org), the national parent club for the Boxer, to learn about the breed from reputable exhibitors and breeders.

Enjoy *Meet the Boxer*!

Sincerely,

Dennis B. Sprung
AKC President and CEO

14

24

112

34

Contents

CHAPTER ONE

The Boxer, Champion of Breeds

Well-conditioned and athletic, the Boxer is a powerful dog with an intelligent and alert expression. Known for their guardian instincts, Boxers love to be with their people. Other breeds may have specialized talents for hunting or herding, but the Boxer is an all-around smart, helpful, and active dog.

When looking for a new pet, you're not considering a Boxer for his historical hunting ability

to chase down and hold a wild boar or bear until the hunter arrived to dispatch it. The breed's origins are fascinating, but few of us today can relate to those dramatic encounters. We can imagine, however, that the Boxer's ancestors that pinned wild boars to the forest floor needed courage, stamina, and determination—three great characteristics for a protector dog to have.

Aside from being such strong guardians, Boxers are also lovebugs, and they make excellent pets for families and fanciers alike. Their acute senses and sweet temperaments qualify them for various service duties, including assistance and therapy work.

BOXER BRIEFS

Many endearing and intriguing qualities characterize the Boxer. Let's explore the many traits that make this resourceful and intelligent dog one of the most popular and recognizable purebred dogs around.

What makes the Boxer so great?

• **Sweet temperament:** A sweet, good-humored, family-oriented dog, the Boxer is trainable and adaptable. The Boxer stands out for the sweetness of his character; a mean Boxer simply should not exist.

• **Devoted family member:** The Boxer thrives with a family. Boxers love their humans, and they are devoted to their families and protect them like their own. They treat children carefully and gently, and obey each family member.

• **Guardian and companion:** Today's Boxer is indeed a stylish companion dog, as well as a guardian. This handsome pup cuts a unique silhouette in dogdom. Whether he's standing proudly in the center ring of a dog show, in your doorway, or in the backyard, the Boxer impresses everyone he encounters.

- **Instinctive protector:** Boxers recognize friends instinctively. Unlike less-discriminating dogs, such as the Golden Retriever and the Beagle, the Boxer does not readily accept everyone as his best friend. When your Boxer backs away from an individual or growls, he is telling you that something is not quite right in the air. Boxers judge character tremendously well.

- **Too smart for their own good:** A dedicated owner who understands the way a Boxer thinks will have few problems training his or her dog, but Boxers tend to ask "why" before they execute a command—especially before they execute a command four or five times simultaneously. Today's Boxers need a bit more patience and incentive to perform obedience work.

- **Ready to serve:** Despite their questioning ways, Boxers are ready to serve. The hundreds of obedience-titled Boxers, highly trained and courageous service dogs, police dogs, and military dogs illustrate the breed's ability to learn and obey commands.

- **Highly adaptable:** Boxers thrive in practically any situation, be it in a family environment, with a retired couple, or with an individual. Because Boxers are so people-oriented, they care very little about their living environments. The Boxer can dwell just as contentedly in an apartment with a terrace (as long as he gets attention and adequate exercise) as he can on a grand estate with a large fenced-in property. He will guard both home and owner with his whole spirit and his whole heart.

- **Lovers, not fighters:** Many breeders will attest that the Boxer rarely
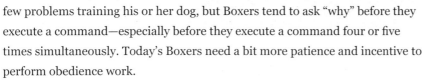
fend his home. Despite all the kissing, the Boxer will fearlessly guard his domain.

Many Boxer fanciers contend that the breed is one you keep—and seek—for life. In fact, quite a few Boxer owners grew up with one or remember having early interactions with the breed during childhood. Having grown up with a Boxer often convinces adults to share one with their own children, and so the legacy continues.

On the other hand, many households without children adopt Boxers because the dogs show similar levels of intelligence as young children, and they are often more obedient! Empty-nesters, too, often welcome Boxers into their homes. The dogs fill the void left by children who have flown the coop, reveling in the attention of their new parents. As Boxer lovers will reveal, a home is not a home without a Boxer.

Did You Know

The Boxer traces his ancestry through a line of dogs known throughout all of Europe—primarily Germany—during the sixteenth century. He is one of many descendents of the old fighting dog of the high valleys of Tibet.

Despite their hunter past, Boxers are full of love and affection. They thrive on human social interaction.

THE WORKING CLASS

The Boxer is classified by the American Kennel Club as a member of the Working group. Dogs in this group were bred to perform a variety of jobs such as guarding property, pulling sleds, and water rescue. For these reasons, Working dogs have

Meet the Boxer

AKC Meet the Breeds®, hosted by the American Kennel Club and presented by PetPartners, Inc., is a great place to see Boxers, as well as more than 200 other dog and cat breeds. Not only can you see dogs, cats, puppies, and kittens of all sizes, you can also talk to experts in each of the breeds. Meet the Breeds features demonstration rings to watch events for law enforcement K9s, grooming, agility, and obedience. You also can browse the more than 100 vendor booths for every imaginable product for you and your pet.

It's great fun for the whole family. AKC Meet the Breeds takes place in the fall in New York City. For more information, check out www.meetthebreeds.com.

been invaluable to mankind throughout time. Intelligent, highly trainable, and quick to learn, these dogs make great companions. However, their strength and large size do not fit just any family. It takes time, patience, and commitment to train the large breeds of the Working group. Other "blue-collar" dogs include the Great Dane, Doberman Pinscher, Rottweiler, Siberian Husky, and Saint Bernard, just to name a few. Boxers today lend a helping hand in a variety of ways, from therapy work to disability assistance to search-and-rescue and bomb detection.

BOREDOM BUSTERS

The intelligent and active Boxer will get bored sitting at home all day with nothing to do. Luckily, there are many things you can do with your dog to help

The Boxer can live in an apartment or condominium, but he loves to get out and stretch his legs. Find a safe dog park in your area to take him to play every week to help expend his energy.

Choosing a Dog Park

When looking for a dog park, be on the lookout for the three *S*'s:

■ **Security.** Gates should be high enough to prevent big dogs from jumping over or small ones from squeezing under; double gates help avert escapes. Some parks provide segregated play areas for large and small dogs. Each area should be clearly designated and fenced.

■ **Sanitation.** Cleaning tools, disinfectant, plastic bags, and trash receptacles should be readily available. All hard surfaces should be disinfected regularly; depending on the amount of dog traffic, this might be daily or weekly.

■ **Safety.** The park should be accessible to emergency services. If the park provides seating for humans, dogs will inevitably jump and climb on it. Make sure the seats are sturdy with slats closely spaced. If the park has no trees, it should have another source of shade. Some dog parks have an on-site water supply; some don't. Either way, water should always be available.

Maintaining and sharing a dog park necessitates courtesy and common sense. Dogs will be dogs, but don't let your pet infringe on anyone's enjoyment of the space. All of the dogs in the park should be adequately supervised to prevent fighting or damage.

promote exercise and good health, not to mention the great bonding opportunity that these activities provide for you and your dog.

Dog parks have become especially popular in urban areas where opportunities for dogs to exercise and socialize are usually limited. Many city parks do not permit dogs on or off leash, so dog parks are great because they provide a safe place for you to let your dog run and play. In the past decade, dog parks have sprung up in many cities. These dog-friendly, securely fenced environments provide a welcome getaway for dogs and dog lovers.

One of the newest trends in the dog park social scene is the breed-specific playdate. Some dog parks feature regular get-togethers where owners of specific breeds meet to socialize, exchange advice, and let their dogs mingle with peers of the same breed. These events are usually publicized through online mailings or breed-related chat lists. Some have become truly gala affairs—featuring birthday celebrations, costume contests, treats, and gifts.

The AKC offers many great sporting activities for you and your dog to participate in together. From conformation to agility to rally to obedience, Boxers excel at them all. If competitive canine sports sound like something you're interested in joining, you'll find further information in chapter 11. So, stay tuned.

THINK ON IT

Getting a dog is a big decision. In good health, a Boxer can live for more than a decade. That's a long-term commitment that you need to be prepared to make. Be sure to discuss this with every member of your family or household before you make a final purchasing decision. It's easy to want to bring home the first cute puppy you see, but make sure the decision is based on what's best for you, your family, and the dog.

Don't let impulse be your guide. Having a dog will greatly affect your everyday life and activities. Once you've done your research on the breed and decide to bring a Boxer into your home, learn all you can about what to expect in the months and years to come. Be prepared, so you can enjoy your future companionship with your new best friend.

At a Glance ...

The Boxer is an intelligent, highly trainable dog with a keen instinct for guardianship.

· ·

Contrary to what you might expect, the breed's calm demeanor suits families with children just fine. The Boxer's all lover, not fighter.

· ·

Because of his intelligence, the Boxer can become defiant and get himself into trouble without your guidance. If you decide to make a Boxer your pet, be sure you have the time, energy, and patience to devote to his training.

CHAPTER TWO

Boxer Basics

The Boxer is a truly splendid sight to behold. This multi-faceted, multi-purpose purebred German breed—designed as a working dog, a protector dog, and a family companion—is the result of generations of selective breeding.

How can you recognize a Boxer? What features define the Boxer "look"? At first glance, it may be the breed's head—the standard states that the chiseled head, with its broad, blunt

The best Boxer resource is the breed's national parent club, the American Boxer Club.

muzzle and correct proportion to the body, gives the breed "a unique individual stamp." A judge in the show ring will first consider the overall balance of the Boxer, a breed that must be of medium size and squarely built with a short back, strong limbs, and a short, tight-fitting coat.

You already know what a Boxer looks like because the breed's many features have drawn your interest. It's the dog's dark, mood-mirroring eyes, his attractive short fawn or brindle coat with those eye-catching white markings, or that unmistakable mug that's both intelligent and imposing enough to scare off an unwanted visitor.

It's indeed the combination of these features that creates the Boxer's unique "look," which is all spelled out in detail in the breed standard. This standard details the physical traits and characteristics seen in a specific breed. It verbally illustrates the physical structure that gives the dog his ability to perform the work he was bred to do. That's where breed clubs come into play.

CLUB AFFILIATIONS

In order for a breed to be recognized by the American Kennel Club, that breed's parent club must organize and provide documentation certifying that its dogs have bred true to form and free from out-crosses for at least five generations. The breed club then develops a written description of what the dog looks like in his most ideal form. Experts of the breed describe physical features of the Boxer like his eyes, ears, nose, jaw, head, body, tail, forequarters, and hindquarters. They also take into account the traits, characteristics, temperament, and jobs that the dog was bred to do.

The Boxer breed's national parent club, the American Boxer Club (ABC), is the gatekeeper for all information related to the breed—tracking health issues,

ABC in the USA

The American Boxer Club, Inc., known as the ABC, has held a national specialty—a show for Boxers only—every year since 1936. The early years of the Boxer fancy in the United States were dominated by great German imports, and the first winner of the specialty was Ch. Corso v Uracher Wasserfall se Sumbula, bred by Karl Walz of Germany. Entries at the first shows only drew around 50 dogs to compete; in time, the show has grown to attract more than 400 Boxers.

promoting responsible breeding programs, and maintaining a social network for fellow fanciers. The ABC wrote the breed standard for the Boxer, essentially providing a detailed description of how the ideal representative of the breed should look, act, and move. This blueprint, so to speak, was then approved and adopted by the AKC for further guidance to all future breeders.

Although the Boxer's original jobs (baiting bulls, boar, or stags) are thankfully nonexistent today, the breed's new jobs (home protector, service dog, and companion) require the same drive, enthusiasm, and ability to learn and obey commands in training. A Boxer's ability to scent (distinguish smells readily), to trot (an efficient movement used to cover long distances that is more comfortable than a gallop), and to work over a period of time and distance, for example, remain things the dog should be able to do readily and with little or no difficulty.

Although the Boxer breed was accepted in the American Kennel Club's registry long ago in 1904, it was another couple of decades before the American Boxer Club was established and accepted, as well. It wasn't until the 1940s that the American public began to take real interest in the breed, which still maintains lofty social standing among its canine peers, holding a spot in the top ten most popular breeds for more than a decade.

FROM HUMBLE BEGINNINGS TO THE JUDGE'S CIRCLE

In order to understand the Boxer we know and love today, it's important that we are familiar with some of this breed's dramatic and rich history. In a time when dogs battled lions, tigers, and other assorted beasts in public arenas, the early Romans chose Mollosus (giant and fierce Mastiff-type dogs) as their fighting breed

The Boxer isn't used for the same bull and boar hunting he was in the past, but the breed still retains its ancestors' strong build and athletic agility.

of choice. They recruited the strongest, most agile and fearless dogs of the litters as warriors, while the remaining pups became guards, protectors, and draft dogs. Boxers trace their lineage back to these ancestors.

Over the centuries and across countries' borders, some of these unqualified dogs were recruited to control savage bulls ready for slaughter. The butchers who owned these dogs bred them to have shorter legs and heavier bodies—better to keep them away from the bull's sharp horns! The Boxer breed developed the most in Germany in the 1800s. Historians credit the famous reputation of a Berlin butcher's dog named "Boxl" for giving the breed its

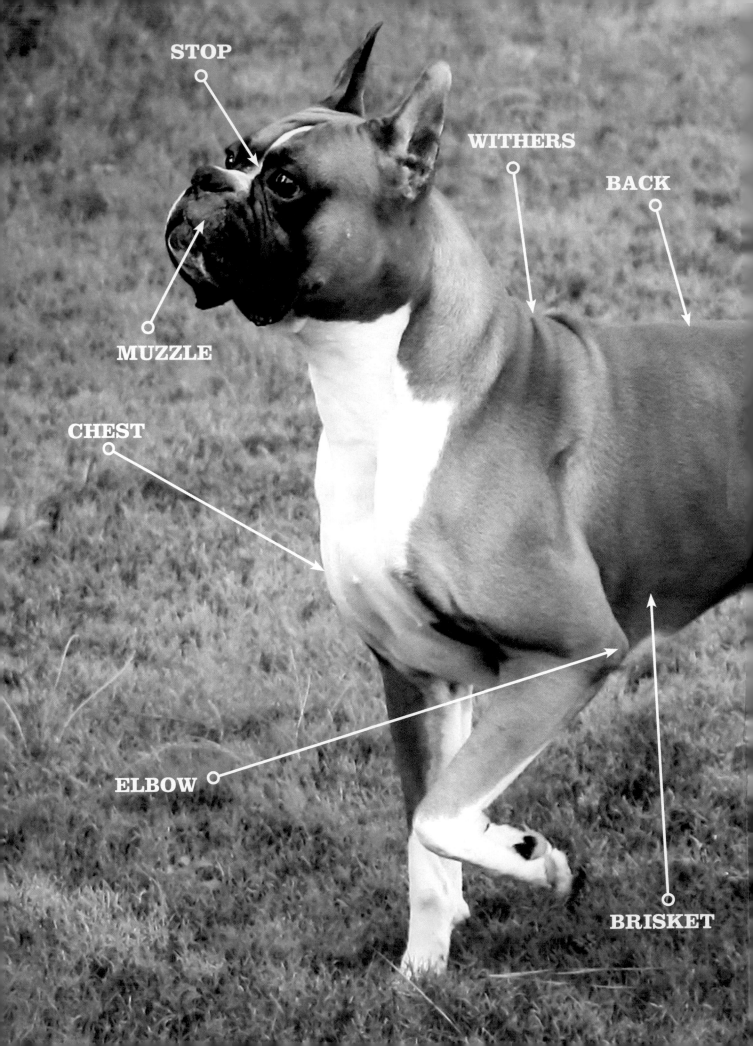

STOP

WITHERS

BACK

MUZZLE

CHEST

ELBOW

BRISKET

Anatomy of a Boxer

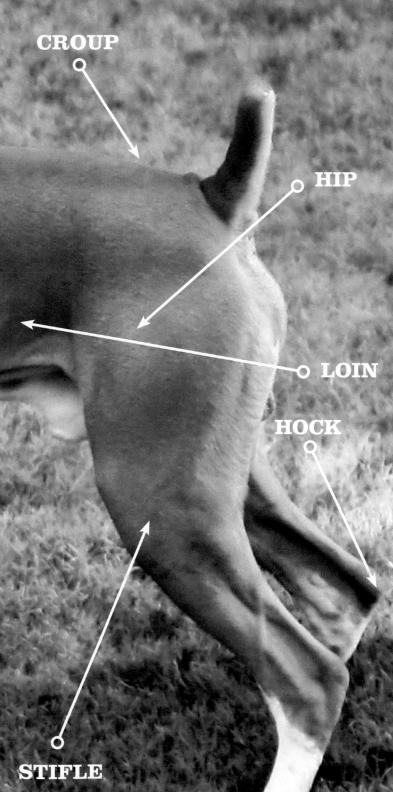

CROUP

HIP

LOIN

HOCK

STIFLE

The Boxer in Brief

COUNTRY OF ORIGIN:
Germany

ORIGINAL PURPOSE:
Bull-baiting and protection

GROUP:
Working

AVERAGE LIFE SPAN:
9 to 11 years

COAT:
Close-fitting and short, shiny and smooth

COLOR:
Fawn, from light tan to mahogany, and brindle, varying in intensity; white marks on the head, chest, and legs, not to exceed one-third of the dog

GROOMING:
Weekly brushing with a hound glove or soft-bristled brush recommended; during shedding season, daily brushing to remove dead hair will help assist new coat growth. Bathe as needed.

TRAINABILITY:
High

PERSONALITY:
A "people" dog, alert and self-assured; basically playful with family and friends, patient and tolerant of children; wary with strangers, but always fearless; loyal, affectionate, and dignified.

ACTIVITY LEVEL:
Moderately high to high; requires daily stimulation and exercise to keep his active mind and body occupied

GOOD WITH OTHER PETS:
Yes, with proper introductions

NATIONAL BREED CLUB:
American Boxer Club
(www.americanboxerclub.org)

RESCUE:
The national club has a list of rescue-related websites on its site, available under "Information."

Not Since Bang Away!

Frau Friederun Miriam Stockmann, the woman credited as the mother of the Boxer breed, traveled from Germany to the United States to see how popular the breed had become. She judged a match and awarded a young fawn Boxer with Best in Match, later describing that winning dog—Ch. Bang Away of Sirrah Crest—as the "best Boxer in America today."

She was right. Many wins later, Ch. Bang Away was crowned Best in Show at Westminster in 1951. In 1952, Bang Away broke the record of 61 Best in Show wins. He retired a content dog with 121 Best in Show wins.

The American dog scene never recovered from the thrill of Bang Away in the 1950s, who appeared on several magazine covers, including *Life, Colliers,* and *Esquire*! Today you can still hear people in the show ring exclaim, "Not since Bang Away!"

name. The word "Boxer" derives from "boxl" or "boxel," which essentially translates into "mutt!"

In the late nineteenth century in Europe, the sport of bull-baiting was born. In a ring, a tethered bull would attempt to impale a dog with its horns. The dog would respond by clamping his vice-like jaws onto the bull's nose, bringing down the beast. The Boxer's lower center of gravity, combined with his unstoppable determination, would eventually force the bull to the ground, where it would bleed to death or die from oxygen deprivation.

These Bullenbeissers, or bull-biters, also hunted wild game, like pig, boar, and deer. Such expeditions often cost the lives of many dogs, as the hunt taxed humans and dogs alike—not to mention the boars!

Despite his humble beginnings in Germany as a boar hunter, the Boxer rose to great fame around the world, including the United States. American breeders have significantly influenced the breed in many countries, with several imports sent to establish new bloodlines and to set the type of the definitive show Boxer.

The first Boxer registered by the American Kennel Club was Arnulf Grandenz in 1904. An American-bred dog, Arnulf was owned by Max H. Schachner in Downers Grove, Illinois. In 1914, Herbert H. Lehman imported Dampf von Dom, a German-bred, award-winning Boxer that became the first American champion for the breed.

A PIECE OF HISTORY

Flemish tapestries of the 16th and 17th centuries depict scenes of stag and boar hunting, featuring ancestors of the Boxer.

Boxer mania began in the 1930s. In 1934, the AKC recorded 71 registered Boxers. The American Boxer Club formed in 1935, signifying the breed's burgeoning popularity. During this time, canine-related sports and hobbies like dog breeding drew more fanciers. In 1936, the ABC held its first specialty show, which was won by Ch. Corso v Uracher Wasserfall se Sumbula, bred by Karl Walz of Germany. By 1938, the number of registered Boxers jumped significantly to 724. You could say fanciers were bitten by the Boxer bug.

It would seem that over the years, the Boxer has traded in his unseemly history in the fighting ring to rule supreme time and again in the show ring.

OWNER SUITABILITY

The Boxer's most notable characteristic is his highly affectionate nature. He loves people and is happiest when he is with his human family. He is playful and known for his stoic patience when playing with children.

Although considered a medium-sized breed, the male Boxer can be rather large, weighing in at 65 to 80 pounds; females tend to weigh a bit less. The adult

Although they are not used for breeding purposes, white Boxers are accepted for AKC registration and participate fully in all performance events. They also make for wonderful household pets.

The Boxer Breed Standard

AMERICAN KENNEL CLUB™

GENERAL APPEARANCE: The ideal Boxer is a medium-sized, square-built dog of good substance with short back, strong limbs, and short, tight-fitting coat. His well-developed muscles are clean, hard, and appear smooth under taut skin. . . . Developed to serve as guard, working, and companion dog, he combines strength and agility with elegance and style. His expression is alert and his temperament steadfast and tractable.

PROPORTION

The body in profile is square.

HEAD

The beauty of the head depends upon the harmonious propor-tion of muzzle to skull. . . . Eyes are dark brown in color, frontally placed, generous, not too small, too protruding, or too deepset. Their mood-mirroring character, combined with the wrinkling of the forehead, gives the Boxer head its unique quality of expressiveness. . . . The ears are customarily cropped, cut rather long and tapering, and raised when alert. If uncropped, the ears should be of moderate size, thin, lying flat and close to the cheeks in repose, but falling forward with a definite crease when alert.

MUZZLE AND NOSE

The top of the muzzle should not slant down, nor should it be concave; however, the tip of the nose should lie slightly higher than the root of the muzzle. The nose should be broad and black.

BITE AND JAW STRUCTURE

The Boxer bite is undershot, the lower jaw protruding beyond the upper and curving slightly upward. . . . Nei-ther the teeth nor the tongue should ever show when the mouth is closed. The lips, which complete the for-mation of the muzzle, should meet evenly in front.

BODY

The chest is of fair width, and the forechest well-defined and visible from the side. The brisket is deep, reaching down to the elbows. . . . The ribs, extending far to the rear, are well-arched but not barrel-shaped. The loins are short and muscular. . . . The tail is set high, docked, and carried upward.

FOREQUARTERS

The shoulders are long and slop-ing, close-lying, and not exces-sively covered with muscle. The upper arm is long, approaching a right angle to the shoulder blade. The elbows should not press too closely to the chest wall nor stand off visibly from it. The forelegs are long, straight, and firmly muscled. . . Feet should be compact, turning neither in nor out, with well-arched toes.

HINDQUARTERS

The hindquarters are strongly muscled, with angu-lation in balance with that of the forequarters. The thighs are broad and curved. . . . Upper and lower thigh are long. The legs are well-angulated at the stifle, with clearly defined, well "let down" hock joints. Viewed from behind, the hind legs should be straight, with hock joints leaning neither in nor out. From the side, the leg below the hock (metatarsus) should be almost perpendicular to the ground. . .

COAT

Short, shiny, lying smooth and tight to the body.

COLOR

The colors are fawn and brindle. . . . White markings, if present, should be of such distribution to enhance the dog's appearance, but may not exceed one-third of the entire coat.

—Excerpts from the Boxer Breed Standard

Boxer is neither nervous nor hyperactive. He can be rambunctious as a youngster and requires training and supervision. Boxers are very trainable but are known for their stubborn streak. Early training during puppyhood is essential in order to develop a healthy relationship between Boxer and owner. Unless the dog learns who is in charge at an early age, he will assume that role himself. A natural guard dog, the Boxer needs obedience instruction to channel his protective instincts. Make sure you're prepared to address these training needs before you decide to bring home a Boxer puppy. If you're not ready to assume these duties, you're not ready to own a Boxer.

Boxers are great with children because of their patient and protective nature. However, all interactions between your Boxer and children should be supervised.

CONSIDER THE BOXER

Despite the breed's past in wild-game hunting, the Boxer truly is a lover at heart. Whip smart and fiercely loyal, he makes a lifelong companion to anyone truly committed to his training and desire for human interaction. To find a training class and other training resources once you've brought your new Boxer home, search the AKC's extensive database for a training club in your area at www.akc .org/events/obedience/training_clubs.

At a Glance ...

The American Boxer Club (ABC), the American Kennel Club's national affiliated breed parent club, is the top resource for all things Boxer-related. The club is the keeper of all information regarding health issues, general care needs, medical advancements, sporting, and other Boxer-related activities—to name a few.

· ·

With care and precision, the ABC has crafted the Boxer breed standard, which details the appearance and temperament of the ideal Boxer.

· ·

A "medium-sized" dog, the Boxer requires daily exercise and (ideally) some yard space to stretch his legs and play throughout the day.

· ·

Boxers have enjoyed decades of success in the show ring. And with some training and dedication from you, yours can, too!

CHAPTER THREE

Your Ideal Boxer Puppy

If you are willing to devote the time, space, patience, and attention that a Boxer rightly deserves, this could be the breed for you! Any Boxer owner will tell you that his dog exudes pride and confidence. Boxers depend on human interaction, thriving on socializing with people, reveling in bestowing affection to their families, and eagerly greeting all friendly visitors.

To prepare for your dog's arrival, the entire family must decide together exactly the type of

pet you want. You'll need to puppy-proof your home and yard, and then do some shopping for puppy essentials. But first things first, do your homework to learn as much as possible about the breed.

You can approach the whole process with greater success if you decide in advance which sex and age suits you and your family's lifestyle. You've already chosen your breed—a Boxer—so now it's time to decide whether you want a male or a female dog, a puppy or an adult.

Don't just bring home the first adorable puppy you see. Take the time to research the Boxer breed's desired traits and characteristics, and check references for breeders.

GUYS AND DOLLS

Like humans, male and female Boxers embody distinct characteristics that make them unique. You'll see these behavioral differences most readily when the dog is not spayed or neutered. Males are loyal and devoted companions, but they will mark their territory. Females don't lift their legs, but they come into heat twice a year, requiring you to guard them from male suitors. Physiologically, Boxer males are slightly larger than females. Other than that, the two genders look identical.

Males

Loving and devoted companions, males tend to maintain a consistent mood, though they can be rowdy and raucous depending on the individual's personality. Intact males will search for females in heat, so they are prone to running off and sowing their wild canine oats. Adolescent males may also challenge and disobey your commands, especially if a female is in the vicinity, so you'll need to add an extra dose of patience during training sessions.

An unaltered male may lift his leg to mark his territory, letting other dogs know that your home and yard is his turf. He will do this regardless of whether he is house-trained, so you'll need to have some odor-busting cleaning products on hand if your Boxer displays this behavior. In altered males, however, this problem is virtually eliminated. They will be less likely to roam, mark their territory, be aggressive, and rebel against your authority. Discuss with your veterinarian the health and behavioral risks and advantages associated with neutering your dog, including some cancers. Unless you plan to breed or show your Boxer, neutering greatly helps reduce pet overpopulation.

Females

Female Boxers make sweet and loyal companions, too. With mother-like instincts, the female dotes on her human family just as she would her canine family.

Unlike their male counterparts, however, intact female Boxers can be moody and temperamental, especially when they come into heat (their fertile period) twice a year. When this happens, you'll need to isolate your dog from ready and willing male suitors.

After your female Boxer is spayed, however, her bossy tendencies will cease (for the most part), and she will settle into a more emotionally constant temperament. Spaying your female Boxer also provides health benefits, as well as behavioral ones. Many dogs kept for pet purposes will benefit from being spayed or neutered. Consult your veterinarian on the topic.

SEARCH FOR THE PERFECT PUPPY

Thanks to the Boxer's continued popularity, you can find purebred puppies from breeders, online, at your local pet store, and through sources listed in consumer magazines. You can even find purebred puppies listed in the newspaper. But keep in mind that cold-calling breeders is the riskiest way to find a pet. By far, the most reliable way to find a quality pet is to find a good breeder, and the best way to find a good breeder is to contact the national or local Boxer club for referrals to breeders in your area. Check out the American Kennel Club (www.akc.org) and the American Boxer Club (www.americanboxerclub.org) websites to help you get started.

The breeders endorsed by the national parent club are required to comply to a code of ethics, which usually includes producing dogs only for breed improvement, having ample time and resources to properly breed and raise puppies, ensuring that all puppies receive necessary socialization and veterinary care, conducting health screenings for breeding stock recommended by the parent club, and selling only healthy and temperamentally stable dogs.

Veterinarians, trainers, groomers, and local dog clubs can also put you in touch with Boxer breeders in your area. Local dog shows are another great way to meet breeders.

But how do you know if a breeder you've found is reputable? How can you be sure the dog you're getting is healthy, is bred from quality parents, and has begun to be socialized? How do you know that your Boxer will be of sound temperament?

Look for upstanding breeders who are experts at selecting, breeding, and preparing dogs for loving homes. Reputable dog breeders seek to preserve and improve the breed that they love. Often, a breeder sticks to rearing one type of dog, is actively involved in the dog fancy and shows his or her dogs at kennel club competitions. A good breeder's goal is to perfect the traits that make the breed unique.

When choosing a breeder, look for someone who:
- ✓ Chooses breeding stock carefully and uses the breed standard as a guide to produce the best puppies possible
- ✓ Tests his or her pups for congenital defects and illnesses
- ✓ Provides proof of health screening, a sales contract, and plenty of references
- ✓ Limits his or her puppy sales to well-qualified homes
- ✓ Asks you questions about your home, your lifestyle, your experience with dogs, and your goals with the puppy
- ✓ Allows you to inspect the breeding facilities and introduces you to the pup's dam (mother) and her litter. Oftentimes, the sire (father) of the

Did You Know?

The Boxer is cousin to practically all recognized breeds of the Bulldog type, all of which go back to basic Molossus breed blood.

Look for a puppy that's social with his littermates and not afraid of interacting with people. A well-socialized puppy will approach without fear.

litter does not live with the breeder, but ask to see photos of the father.

CHOOSING YOUR BOXER

A healthy puppy or adult Boxer should be lively and energetic, happy to see you, and willing to approach you without fear. Regardless of where you get him, he should be as healthy as possible when you bring him home. You want your Boxer to begin his life with you as a sound, well-adjusted pup without obvious physical or behavioral flaws.

You also want to choose a Boxer that exemplifies the breed's standard. Look for a handsome Boxer that is the picture of good health; find a pedigree that indicates the dog's parents come from long-lived bloodlines.

A Healthy Puppy

Start looking for signs of good health the moment you start shopping for puppies. Don't just fall in love with the first adorable pup you see—because they're all adorable. For that matter, it's probably best to leave your children (and maybe even your checkbook) at home during your preliminary search.

If the puppy you're considering is still with his littermates, look at the whole group. They should all be active and playful. If all the puppies appear sound, take a closer look at each pup individually. Here are some signs of good health to look for:

• **Eyes, ears, and gums:** The pups should all have clear, bright eyes with no redness or discharge; cold, damp noses; and clean ears with no signs of ear mites (signs of ear mites include head shaking, ear scratching, and specks of dark brown material in the ears). The puppies' ears should be odor-free, and their gums should look pink and healthy.

• **Body:** The puppies' coats should be shiny and clean, and their skin should appear pink and healthy, with no hot spots or sores. Their bodies should appear full, firm, and muscular. Their bellies should not be bloated, which could be a sign of worms.

• **Disposition:** Behavior matters when choosing a pup. You want an alert Boxer that leaps up to see you, wagging his little tail in sheer ecstasy. You don't, however, want a pup that appears overly aggressive or domineering—or a shy, submissive pup that hides in the corner or appears listless. Stick with a puppy with a more even temperament: excited but not giddy, laid-back but not listless. Shy or easily spooked temperaments are also less than desirable.

If the breeder okays it, take the puppy into an area where he hasn't been before. Then put him down and watch his reaction. If he follows you, he is eager

A lively and energetic puppy makes for a lively and energetic adult dog. Look for a Boxer pup that likes to run around and play when you visit him at the breeder.

A Healthy Adult

A healthy adult dog should embody these features:

- Clear, bright eyes with no redness, discharge, or injuries
- A cold, wet nose with no discharge of any kind
- Clean, erect ears with no signs of ear mites or infection
- Clean and bright teeth with little tartar
- A smooth, clean coat free from external parasites, including fleas, ticks, and mange
- Healthy, pink skin with no sores
- An overall sound structure with healthy legs, paws, and body
- No signs of coughing, congestion, or diarrhea
- Free and easy movement with no difficulty moving about
- Well-socialized, appearing confident and not afraid of sudden sounds or movements
- Up to date on all shots and vaccinations

to please. If he chooses to explore his surroundings, he's a curious pup that may have a short attention span. All the different reactions help to reveal the Boxer puppy's true personality.

THE RIGHT CONFORMATION

Whether you choose a puppy or an adult, your Boxer should reflect—or come close to reflecting—the breed standard. Here are some traits to look for when selecting your soon-to-be best friend:

- **Color:** Choose a puppy with deep, rich pigmentation. In selecting a fawn-colored dog, seek a deep-red coat, especially down the back and head; in a brindle dog, look for distinctive herringbone striations against a deep-red background. White markings may be present on the chest, legs, forehead, and muzzle.
- **Nose and muzzle:** By six to ten weeks of age, the Boxer's nose should appear well pigmented and broad. His muzzle should be broad and deep, making him look expressive as an adult.
- **Eyes:** Dark eyes are best. Boxer pups tend to have bluish eyes that darken as they age. Look for expression in your puppy's eyes, as this signifies intelligence.
- **Gait:** Note the way that your favorite puppy moves. Even in puppyhood, Boxers should show clean movement with no tendency to stumble or drag their hind feet, although Boxers' movement can appear awkward during their puppy months.
- **Structure:** The pup's topline should be as straight as possible, with the shoulders sloping and the back short. Avoid toplines that roach (rise notably) toward the center. And keep an eye out for weak rear quarters and poor feet.
- **Bite and jaw:** The puppy's bite should be somewhat undershot, meaning the lower jaw protrudes farther than the upper jaw. The puppy's lower jaw should be as wide as possible, which is ideal for incoming adult teeth.

RESCUING AN ADULT

An adult Boxer can be a delight, too. He will have graduated from that awkward puppy stage into adulthood, rendering him more manageable and independent. Depending on the dog's history and training skills, you won't have to send him to basic obedience classes or house-train him. He's simply ready to be your constant companion.

Because of the Boxers' adaptability, an adult makes an excellent choice for a family that wants a dog but doesn't want to endure challenging puppy behaviors, like house-training, obedience training, and chewing.

You can find adult Boxers in a variety of ways:

• **Kennel clubs and breeders:** Boxer breeders can be an excellent source for finding an adoptable adult dog, and kennel clubs can help put you in touch with these breeders. Many times, breeders have adult males or females that they

Get Your Registration and Pedigree

A responsible breeder will be able to provide your family with an American Kennel Club registration and pedigree.

AKC REGISTRATION: When you buy a Boxer puppy from a breeder, ask the breeder for an American Kennel Club Dog Registration Application form. The breeder will fill out most of the application for you. When you fill out your portion of the document and mail it to the AKC, you will receive a Registration Certificate proving that your Boxer is officially part of the AKC. Besides recording your name and your dog's name in the AKC database, registration helps fund the AKC's good works such as canine health research, search-and-rescue teams, educating the public about responsible dog care, and much more.

CERTIFIED PEDIGREE: A pedigree is an AKC certificate proving that your dog is a purebred Boxer. It shows your puppy's family tree, listing the names of his parents and grandparents. If your dog is registered with the AKC, the organization will have a copy of your dog's pedigree on file, which you can order from its website (www.akc.org). Look for any titles that your Boxer's ancestors have won, including any AKC dog shows, competitions, or certifications. A pedigree doesn't guarantee the health or good personality of a dog, but it's a starting point for picking out a good Boxer puppy.

There are plenty of adult Boxers that need good, loving homes. If you want to open your home and heart to one, contact a Boxer rescue group.

no longer use for breeding or that have developed flaws that no longer allow them to compete in conformation shows. Often, after dogs are past their reproductive stages, breeders place Boxers in loving homes so they can enjoy the rest of their lives being spoiled by loving owners. Sometimes, a breeder will also have an adult dog that was returned because the owner was no longer able to care for him. These dogs make fine companions, and you can be sure that they have been well cared for.

• **Breed-specific rescue organizations:** You can also find adult Boxers through rescue organizations that specialize in finding homes for dogs whose owners are no longer able to care for them. Most rescue groups require that you complete an application, and you will be interviewed by a representative of the organization. When you're approved for an adoption, you'll be placed on a waiting list and notified when a dog is available. After the dog moves in with you, the organization will likely follow up to be sure the dog is settling in well. Because the goal of these rescue groups is to find forever homes for all of the animals taken in, members of these organizations will take extra time and care to ensure that the dogs are successfully adopted to owners who understand and value the long-term commitment.

If you decide to adopt an adult dog, remember that you're saving a Boxer's life. Most people gravitate toward puppies, but adults need homes, too, and you can feel good about giving a dog a second chance at life.

TAKE SOME ADVICE

Listen to your breeder; a good one will do more than just breed cute puppies. He or she can also help you pick out the best pup from the litter to fit your lifestyle and

Responsible Pet Ownership

AMERICAN
KENNEL CLUB™

Getting a dog is exciting, but it's also a huge responsibility. That's why it's important to educate yourself on all that is involved in being a good pet owner. As a part of the Canine Good Citizen® test, the AKC has a "Responsible Dog Owner's Pledge," which states:

I will be responsible for my dog's health needs.

☐ I will provide routine veterinary care, including check-ups and vaccines.

☐ I will offer adequate nutrition through proper diet and clean water at all times.

☐ I will give daily exercise and regularly bathe and groom.

I will be responsible for my dog's safety.

☐ I will properly control my dog by providing fencing where appropriate, by not letting my dog run loose, and by using a leash in public.

☐ I will ensure that my dog has some form of identification when appropriate (which may include collar tags, tattoos, or microchip identification).

☐ I will provide adequate supervision when my dog and children are together.

I will not allow my dog to infringe on the rights of others.

☐ I will not allow my dog to run loose in the neighborhood.

☐ I will not allow my dog to be a nuisance to others by barking while in the yard, in a hotel room, etc.

☐ I will pick up and properly dispose of my dog's waste in all public areas, such as on the grounds of hotels, on sidewalks, in parks, etc.

☐ I will pick up and properly dispose of my dog's waste in wilderness areas, on hiking trails, on campgrounds, and in off-leash parks.

I will be responsible for my dog's quality of life.

☐ I understand that basic training is beneficial to all dogs.

☐ I will give my dog attention and playtime.

☐ I understand that owning a dog is a commitment in time and caring.

personality. If you know you want to compete with your Boxer, be sure to tell the breeder ahead of time. He or she can help you pick out the desired characteristics you'll need for success. A show-bound puppy may cost more than a pet, but not necessarily, so trust the breeder's advice in selecting a pup with the most show-ring potential. After all, no one knows these puppies and their lineage better. As long as you are honest with your breeder about your lifestyle, intentions for your pet, and your own personal dog-owning experience, the breeder will lead you to the right puppy for you!

At a Glance ...

Boxers are highly social. They thrive on interaction with the people they love.

· ·

There are some distinct differences between male and female Boxers—mainly related to personality and size. Discuss these differences with the breeder when deciding which dog is right for you.

· ·

If you're serious about your search for a Boxer puppy that is a good representation of the breed, look for a reputable breeder to purchase one from. A healthy, happy dog is worth the money.

· ·

Utilize the breeder's wealth of information on the topic of Boxers. After all, no one knows the puppies in the litter better. If you are clear and up-front about what purposes you want your dog for, the breeder will be able to help you select the best dog from the litter to suit your needs.

· ·

Adult Boxers make for sweet pets, too; not to mention the added benefit of skipping over house-training woes. There are many rescue organizations dedicated to finding permanent homes for adult Boxers; contact one if adopting an adult Boxer is something you'd like to do.

CHAPTER FOUR

Your Boxer's New Home

You've chosen your Boxer, and he's ready to come home. Great! Before he arrives, you want to be certain that everything in your home is ready for the new addition. Much like baby-proofing, you will need to puppy-proof your home to ensure that it is safe *for* your puppy and safe *from* your puppy. Plus, you'll need to stock up on all the necessary equipment your puppy will need during his first few weeks at home. Make a shopping list and hit

the store early, so you're well prepared by the time your Boxer is ready to transition from the breeder's home to yours.

PUPPY-PROOFING YOUR HOME AND YARD

You must prepare your home and yard for a new puppy just as you would for a curious toddler. Look at the world from your Boxer's perspective—about 3 feet off the ground—and pay particular attention to the following areas:

• **Kitchen:** The kitchen contains all sorts of interesting drawers, cabinets, and cords, not to mention the tempting smells of food and trash. Childproof latches, which can be found at your local hardware store, prevent curious pups from investigating, and they keep potentially dangerous foods and cleaning supplies behind secured cabinet doors and drawers. Tuck power cords out of reach or enclose them in chew-proof PVC tubing to avoid giving your dog a shock.

Be diligent about putting away leftovers rather than leaving them on the counter where your dog can reach them. Secure the garbage can with a locking lid or store it behind a latched cabinet door to keep the rubbish inside the can—not all over the kitchen floor!

• **Bathroom:** Razors, pills, cotton swabs, and soap left within your dog's reach can be easily ingested, which can result in an expensive emergency vet visit. All family members need to be conscientious about cleaning up after themselves in the bathroom.

As with the kitchen, use a trash can with a locking lid, or stash the trash under the sink. Also install childproof latches on the drawers and cabinets, and be sure to tuck dangling cords away and out of your Boxer's reach.

• **Bedroom:** Dogs are scent-oriented, so they gravitate toward anything that smells like you. Shoes, slippers, and clothing will quickly become toys if you don't safeguard them behind a closed closet door. Keep clothing picked up, store

Consider the Microchip

In addition to a dog collar, you should also think about having your veterinarian insert a microchip in your dog to help find him if he ever gets lost. When scanned, the microchip will show your dog's unique microchip number so that your Boxer can be returned to you as soon as possible. Go to www .akccar.org to learn more about the nonprofit American Kennel Club Companion Animal Recovery (AKC CAR) pet recovery system.

Since 1995, the AKC CAR recovery service has been selected by millions of dog owners who are grateful for the peace of mind and service that AKC CAR offers. Learn more at www.akccar.org.

shoes out of reach, and put laundry in a tall, closed hamper. Also store jewelry, hair ties, coins, and other small ingestible items in containers or drawers, and secure any exposed cords or wires.

• **Office:** Your office is filled with temptations: papers, magazines, cords, wires, paper clips, rubber bands, and staples. These items can be fatal if chewed or swallowed. As with the rest of the house, pick up strewn office supplies, secure or enclose cords and wires, and keep decorative items well out of your Boxer's reach. An alternative is to keep the door to the office shut whenever your dog is in the house.

• **Outdoor hazards:** When you look around your garage and yard, you'll see many obvious and not-so-obvious dangers to your Boxer. Put away paint, cleaners, and insecticides. Plant precious (or poisonous) plants behind fences or in areas that your dog cannot access. Store tools and gardening equipment out of your pup's reach. Sniffing a sharp blade could slice his nose, or tugging on a cord may cause a heavy saw to fall and break one of his bones, or worse.

SHOPPING FOR YOUR BOXER

Shopping for your Boxer can be an intimidating experience—but it's also fun! Walk through any pet-supply store, and you'll see aisles of premium food and treats, plush beds, and toys of every shape and size. To begin with, pick up a few necessary items to make your Boxer's homecoming smooth. Brands, quality, and costs run the gamut. Shop around, but don't sacrifice quality for price.

Leashes and collars

Your Boxer will need a collar, leash, and possibly a harness soon after you bring him home. A collar does so much more than simply make a fashion statement; it also holds your dog's license and ID tags, which lists your contact information should your dog ever get lost. The collar also attaches to the leash, which you will need to walk your Boxer.

• **Collar:** For your dog's first few collars, pick up an adjustable nylon one with a buckle. These collars come in a variety of colors and styles to fit your Boxer's personality. To find the right size, measure the diameter of your Boxer's neck, and add 2 inches for some growing room, or take your dog to the pet store and try some on him. Plan to buy several collars as your pup grows. After your Boxer is fully grown, collar choices are endless. Whatever collar you choose, be sure that it's sized and weighted appropriately for your Boxer.

• **Leash:** The dog's leash, which attaches to the collar, gives you control during walks or obedience training. When you purchase a leash, make sure the

Buy your Boxer a collar that fits around his neck with 2 inches to spare, so he has a little room to grow.

attachment won't break or unhook from the collar, and choose one with a strong and comfortable loop for your hand. For your Boxer's first leash, get a 4-foot nylon, cotton webbing, or leather variety. As you begin obedience training, you'll need longer leashes, including 6-foot and 15-foot lengths.

● **Harness:** You can also choose a harness for your Boxer. Rather than encircling your dog's neck like a collar, a harness loops around his shoulders and torso. Once the dog steps into it, you simply snap or buckle it closed. The leash attaches to the back of the harness instead of the collar, putting the pressure around the dog's body instead of his neck. This is especially helpful for dogs with esophageal problems.

Tags, Tattoos, and Microchips

Your Boxer will require some identification, and you can choose from several options: ID tags, tattoos, and microchips. They each have their benefits and drawbacks, so the best option is to use a combination of at least two.

A PIECE OF HISTORY

Although the Boxer breed reached its greatest perfection in Germany during the past hundred years, the breed's ancestry springs from a line of dogs known throughout the whole of Europe since the 16th century.

It's a Wild World

Unexpected noises or unusual experiences can scare a puppy. If he develops fear toward a particular sound or activity, it may stick with him for life. To prevent your Boxer from becoming a scaredy-cat, expose him to a variety of potentially frightening things.

IN THE HOUSE:

- A cookie sheet being dropped on the floor
- The sight and sound of a rolling ball
- A plastic garbage bag snapping open
- A paper bag being crumpled
- A broom and mop in use
- Children's toys, especially those that make noise
- The roar of the vacuum cleaner
- The sounds of a dishwasher, garbage disposal, and trash compactor in use
- The tumbling noises of the washing machine and dryer

OUTSIDE:

- A revving car engine
- A garbage truck in front of the house
- A motorcycle zipping by
- Kids on bikes, skateboards, and rollerblades

IN THE BACKYARD:

- The lawn mower
- A weed whacker and leaf blower
- A rake or other tools
- Metal and plastic trash cans, including the lids

IN ADDITION, HELP HIM WITH:

- Walking up and down stairs
- Walking over a wooden footbridge
- Walking over a manhole cover
- Riding on an elevator
- Walking on different surfaces, including carpet, artificial turf, slippery floors, and rubber mats

Common Household Poisons

Many items that you use every day in your home and yard can be toxic to dogs. They can cause rashes, vomiting, diarrhea, or worse. As you're puppy-proofing your home, put these products out of your dog's reach.

- Acetaminophen
- Antifreeze
- Bleach
- Boric acid
- Car fluids
- Cleaning fluids
- Deodorizers
- Detergents
- Disinfectants
- Drain cleaners
- Furniture polish
- Gasoline
- Herbicides
- Insecticides
- Kerosene
- Matches
- Mothballs
- Nail polish and remover
- Paint
- Prescription medication
- Rat poison
- Rubbing alcohol
- Snail or slug bait
- Turpentine

- **ID tags:** Readily visible on your dog's collar, ID tags list information about your dog and you, such as your Boxer's name and your name, address, and telephone number. At the very least, list your name and the best way to contact you, whether it's your cell phone, office phone, or home phone. If you have several collars for your Boxer, be sure each one has an ID tag.

ID tags can fall off, or sometimes the engraving wears off, so regularly check the ID tag to make sure it's still attached to the collar and is readable. Replace it or update the contact information when necessary.

- **Tattoos:** Tattoos are another identification option. An authorized artist, generally recommended by your veterinarian or breeder, will tattoo a unique number on your Boxer's skin, typically on his belly or inner thigh. A virtually painless procedure, the tattoo is done in minutes.

The number can be any sequence you choose: the dog's AKC number, a random number selected by the tattoo registry, or even your birthday. The number is then listed with one of several national tattoo databases. When your dog is found, the shelter contacts the various registries and matches the tattoo number to you.

   • **Microchips:** A rice-sized microchip is another method of identifying your Boxer. Injected by your veterinarian between your dog's shoulder blades, this microchip contains a code that is stored with your contact information in a database. When your dog is found, a staff member at the shelter uses a hand-held scanner to read the code in the microchip. The code is then entered into the database, which tells the shelter your name and phone number, so you and your dog can be reunited.

   If you have your dog microchipped, take the time to register your contact information and keep it up to date. The microchip won't do any good if there's no name or phone number associated with it, or if the information is incorrect! Similarly, if you move or change your phone number, notify the registry and update your information as necessary.

Bowls and Dishes

Your Boxer will need food and water bowls when he comes home. These doggy dishes vary from custom-painted ceramic ware and hand-thrown pottery to sleek, stainless-steel bowls and durable plastic dishes. Each material has its benefits and drawbacks:

   • **Plastic:** Bowls and dishes made of plastic are lightweight and inexpensive, but they retain residue and harbor bacteria as they get scratched and cracked. If you choose plastic, purchase a hard, dishwasher-safe plastic and replace it at the first signs of wear.

   • **Ceramic:** Ceramic pieces weigh more than plastic dishes, so they're not likely to tip over or become chew toys. However, these dishes are more expensive, and they break easily; if they're made overseas, they may contain lead, which can be harmful to your Boxer.

   • **Stainless steel:** Stainless-steel bowls, though usually the most expensive, clean and sanitize easily. They're heavy enough that your dog won't wander off with one, and they're virtually indestructible. Some designs include rubber bases to keep them from sliding across the floor as your Boxer scarfs down his dinner.

   Your Boxer will need at least two sets of bowls (two for food and two for water) that you can rotate so you can wash them regularly. The bowl size will grow as your Boxer—and his appetite—grows.

Gate, Pens, and Crates

A must for any puppy owner, containment devices of all sorts keep your Boxer in a confined area where you can monitor and house-train him. You will need a dog crate or carrier, and an X-pen, a playpen, or gates when you bring your Boxer home.

   • **Crates:** Crates and kennels come in a variety of sizes and materials, including plastic, nylon, powder-coated wire, and stainless steel. The hard-sided plastic and fiberglass models, which are generally lighter and more portable, frequently double as airline-approved carriers (check with your airline to be certain). The wire and stainless-steel varieties allow for more air flow during hot summer weather, but they don't provide the privacy your Boxer may want.

Your dog should be able to stand up, turn around, lie down, and stretch out in his kennel. Boxers enjoy a cozy den-like area rather than a wide-open space. Although you may want to give your Boxer an entire room of his own, dogs actually prefer to feel enclosed in their crates. Plus, the more space you provide in the crate, the more likely your dog will eliminate in one area and sleep in another.

• **X-pens:** An X-pen is a set of portable wire panels that confines your pup to a specific area. You can adjust it to fit any space. After you have assembled the pen, you can enclose your pup, his crate, food and water bowls, and toys inside the space. Playpens, much like those for human babies, serve a similar purpose.

• **Gates:** Household gates will give your Boxer a little more freedom inside the house. They confine your pup to one room or one part of the house, keeping the rest off limits. Gates easily attach to door frames, and you can remove them whenever you want.

Heavy-duty ceramic or stainless-steel food and water bowls can withstand the wear and tear your Boxer will put them through.

Food and Treats

When it comes to food and treats for your Boxer, you can choose from countless diets and menus. From crunchy fortified kibble and canned stews to organic blends fit for human consumption, pet-food manufacturers roll out hundreds of healthy diets for dogs. Treats, too, come in a range of flavors and styles.

• **Food:** As a puppy, your Boxer requires food formulated for growth and development. It contains more essential nutrients, such as protein and carbohydrates, which encourage the growth of healthy bones and muscles. When he's an adult, he should eat food designed for maintenance. These diets pack less of a punch than the puppy formula, but they still provide everything your Boxer needs to be healthy.

Selecting the right food can be daunting. You can feed the same diet that the breeder fed to your Boxer, or you can talk with your veterinarian about the right diet for your dog. Keep in mind, however, that your Boxer will do much of the choosing; if he doesn't like the taste, he'll let you know! See chapter 8 for more information about selecting the proper diet for your Boxer.

• **Treats:** When purchasing treats, note the ingredients and nutritional information so that you know exactly what you're feeding your pup. Though you'll be tempted to treat your Boxer often, remember that these are treats—not meals. Too many goodies can spoil your pup's appetite or lead to a weight issue. It's best to opt for healthier treats that are low in calories.

Boxer Bedding

Everyone loves a comfy bed, and Boxers are no exception. While you're house-training your Boxer, you may have him sleep in his crate or kennel. Smaller beds and bumper beds covered in fleece or sheepskin are designed just for this purpose. They keep the dog warm and cozy while he's sleeping the night—or day—away.

After your Boxer is house-trained and graduates from his crate to a real dog bed, you can choose from all shapes and sizes. As with the other Boxer essentials, purchase a bed that is sized appropriately for your dog.

Grooming Goodies

Your Boxer's coat requires regular washing and brushing. He also needs his nails trimmed, his ears cleaned, and his teeth brushed. Flip to chapter 7 for details on grooming, but here's a list of primping products to put together a grooming starter kit to have ready before your Boxer comes home:

- Bristle brush
- Cotton balls
- Ear-cleaning solution
- Hair dryer
- Nail clippers
- Shampoo and conditioner
- Slicker brush
- Small scissors
- Styptic powder for nail-clipping accidents
- Toothbrush and toothpaste
- Towel

PLAYTIME!

Like every other section in the pet store, the toy aisle seems endless. From squeaky balls to colorful ropes, stuffed animals, and treat-stuffing hard rubber balls, there's a toy available for any dog's preference.

Despite all the choices, only offer your Boxer toys that are sized appropriately for him. Imagine your 60-pound Boxer shredding a plush toy designed for a Yorkshire Terrier or accidentally choking on a tiny dog bone! Choose toys that are strong, durable, and well made. To ensure your pet's safety, check all toys for potential hazards, such as small pieces that can fall off and cause gastric problems if ingested.

CLEANUP DUTY

Cleaning up after your dog is one of the necessary evils of pet ownership. When your Boxer is a puppy (and every now and then after he's an adult), you'll need to clean up indoor potty accidents. You also need to clean up his bathroom area outside. Luckily, many different products cater specifically to this dirty job.

You can find a variety of cleaners, including those formulated to neutralize pet odors, in most pet-supply stores. Look for a product that not only cleans up the accident, but also eliminates all traces of its occurrence. Enzyme-based cleaners are key in this regard. They break down the chemical compounds of the waste elements, ensuring that your dog won't return to eliminate in the same spot time and again.

Pooper scoopers, a cleanup necessity for picking up your puppy's poop, range from high-tech gadgets to the simple shovel and rake. These days, you can

Keep your Boxer handsome with regular grooming, which includes brushing, bathing, clipping his nails, and brushing his teeth.

also find cleanup bags in various sizes, shapes, and materials, including biodegradable varieties. Always take a cleanup bag (or simply use a plastic grocery bag) on long walks in the park or through the neighborhood with your Boxer. Nobody likes dog walkers, who leave their messes for someone else to find and deal with.

DON'T FORGET YOUR DOG'S LICENSE …

Depending on where you live, county or state laws require that your dog be licensed. The dog-licensing agency issues an identification number, along with a dog tag bearing the number that your Boxer is to wear at all times.

To apply for a dog license, contact your local animal-control agency, and you will receive a form asking for your name, address, and phone number, as well as your pet's name, breed, sex, age, microchip number (if applicable), and whether your Boxer has been spayed or neutered. The agency may also require a copy of your dog's rabies vaccination and sterilization certificate.

Upon approval of your documentation, you will receive a license tag with a unique number that should be attached to your dog's collar. If your Boxer makes a run for it, there's a good chance that he will be picked up and returned to you if he is wearing his collar and tag.

Young Pup Must-Haves

Besides a crate, toys, food, and other essential items listed in this chapter, puppy owners need some specific items to help them through this fascinating time of development.

House-training pads: House-training pads are absorbent sheets lined with plastic, and they prevent mistakes from soiling your floor.

Bumper pad or bed: A bumper pad fits inside the crate, giving your baby Boxer a comfortable place to rest.

Pup-sized toys: Because adult toys are too big for small pups, you need small plush or rope toys sized just for them. Pick toys that don't have sharp edges or removable parts that can be swallowed.

Chewing deterrents: Puppies will chew—it's to be expected. If your Boxer develops a penchant for the corner of your couch, you can spray chewing deterrents, like bitter apple spray, on the area to discourage the behavior.

Gentle shampoo: A puppy's coat and skin can be sensitive, so pick a shampoo and conditioner formulated just for puppies.

... AND HIS REGISTRATION

You should also register your dog with the American Kennel Club. The process begins with the breeder, who first registers his or her dog's litter. When you take ownership of the puppy, the breeder will give you a dog registration application to complete and mail to the AKC. You can do this before or after you bring your Boxer home, but it must be done before the pup reaches his first birthday.

To register your Boxer, you need to fill out the application jointly with the breeder, who provides the dog's sex, color and markings, transfer date, your name and address, and the breeder's signature.

You provide the dog's name, payment information, registration options, and your signature. The AKC charges a nominal nonrefundable registration fee. When the application and fees are approved, you will receive an official certificate of registry.

Even dogs that have mastered house-training will have the occasional accident indoors. Always have the proper cleaning supplies on hand.

At a Glance ...

Prepare a puppy preparedness shopping list and go to the pet-supply store before you bring your new Boxer home. Immediately, he'll need everything from food and bowls to bedding and a crate to identification, collar, and leash. Don't wait until the moment you need something to run out to the store to buy it.

. . . .

Puppy-proof your home much the same as you would for a toddler. Get on your Boxer's level to see what potential dangers lurk around your home.

. . . .

License and registration are two important pieces of paper to get for your puppy when you first bring him home.

CHAPTER FIVE

Early Education

When you first bring your Boxer home, give him a little time to get used to his new family and his surroundings. Once he's comfortable in his new home, start socializing your Boxer by introducing him to different people, places, sounds, smells, and situations. You can also begin his early training. Don't overwhelm your puppy with too many new things at the same time. Make his introductions slowly and in stress-free

Pup Meets World

Thorough socialization includes not only meeting new people and other pets, but also being introduced to new experiences, like riding in the car, having his coat brushed, hearing the television, and walking in a crowd.

The more your pup experiences—and the more positive those experiences are—the less of a shock and the less frightening new situations will be for your Boxer as he grows older.

environments. Once your puppy has completed his vaccinations, you can enroll him in a basic training or puppy kindergarten class, which is a great way for him to meet other dogs and learn the basics of good canine behavior.

SAFE, SOCIAL INTERACTION

After your puppy comes home, wait a couple of weeks, then introduce him to as many people as possible. You're a proud new puppy parent; it's only natural that you want to show him off! Exposure to others helps your dog learn to accept and not be fearful of most people.

Trainers recommend that your pup meet and be handled by at least 100 people of all different ages, sizes, and ethnicities during the first few months of his life! Diversity is the key. Your Boxer should meet people with glasses, hats, mustaches and beards, as well as people who use wheelchairs and canes. He should meet the children down the street, the teenagers next door, and the retired seniors across the way. The more variety he experiences, the better.

Your veterinarian will probably tell you not to take your Boxer out until he has been fully vaccinated. That may be easier said than done, but your puppy's health is the priority! Avoid interactions with other dogs until your Boxer's final round of vaccinations is completed, but start introductions with people you know well as soon as your new pup appears to be acclimated to his new family and surroundings.

Make Your Puppy a S.T.A.R.

The American Kennel Club has a great program for new puppy owners called the S.T.A.R. Puppy Program, which is dedicated to rewarding puppies that get off to a good start by completing a basic training class. S.T.A.R. stands for: Socialization, Training, Activity, and Responsibility.

You must enroll in a six-week puppy training course with an AKC-approved evaluator. When the class is finished, the evaluator will test your puppy on all the training taught during the course, such as being free of aggression toward people and other puppies in the class, tolerating a collar or body harness, allowing his owner to take away a treat or toy, and sitting and coming on command.

If your puppy passes the test, he will receive a certificate and a medal. You and your puppy will also be listed in the AKC S.T.A.R. Puppy records. To learn more about the AKC S.T.A.R. Puppy Program or to find an approved evaluator near you, check out www.akc.org/starpuppy.

Try these tips for keeping your Boxer social, yet safe. Start slowly; stick to your house during the first week or two, then expand from there.

- **Take him with you wherever you go.** Dress him in a pup-sized collar with an ID tag, attach a matching leash, and let him shadow you as you go on quick trips to the market, the coffee shop, or a friend's house.

- **Let him meet as many people as possible.** Introduce him to your neighbors, the postal carrier, and the pet-store cashier. Wherever you go, you and your adorable pup will create a stir. The more people he meets, the better he'll adjust.

- **Invite friends to your house and play pass-the-pup.** By meeting people on his own turf, your Boxer develops confidence as well as social skills. And as each person handles your Boxer, he gets used to being touched by different humans—all with different smells and appearances.

- **Host a Boxer meet-and-greet with other dog owners:** After your Boxer has had his vaccinations, invite other Boxers and their owners over for a puppy playdate, but make sure their dogs have had their shots, too. Always supervise all interactions, especially if the dogs are older or larger than your pup.

START YOUR TRAINING RIGHT

For your Boxer to realize his full potential, he will require obedience and behavior training. Unless you're a dog trainer or an experienced dog owner, it's likely that you don't know much about training a dog. A dog is not a little human; you can't reason with him, you can't talk him into behaving a certain way, and you can't ground him for bad behavior. The only thing he knows is how to act like a dog. So as his owner, you need to communicate with him in a way that he'll understand.

Your Boxer wants nothing more than to find his place in your family. If you don't assert yourself as leader, he'll assume that role—something you don't want

Introduce your Boxer to many new people and situations to avoid fear and aggression as he grows older.

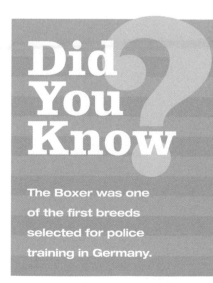

Did You Know?

The Boxer was one of the first breeds selected for police training in Germany.

to happen. Your job is to communicate clearly and firmly how you want him to behave through positive reinforcement.

LEARNING TO OBEY CUES

The old adage "You can't teach an old dog new tricks" may be true in some cases, but dogs of any age can learn how to obey basic cues.

Puppies pick up cues quickly, which results in a high success rate in developing well-mannered and well-adjusted adult dogs. Training a Boxer puppy is like working with a dry sponge in a pool of water: the pup soaks up whatever you show him and constantly looks for more things to do and learn.

With more patience, an older dog can produce similar results as puppies. From six months on, these budding adolescent dogs start to produce hormones,

Training Tips

Successful puppy training depends on several important principles:

1. Use simple one-word cues and say them only once. Otherwise, your Boxer will learn that "come" (or "sit" or "down") is a three- or four-word cue.

2. Never correct your dog for something he did a few minutes earlier. He won't remember what he did wrong. Correct him in the act.

3. Always praise (and offer a treat) as soon as he does something good (or when he stops doing something bad). How else will your Boxer know he's a good dog?

4. Be consistent. You can't play on the bed together today, but then tell him it's wrong to cavort on the bed tomorrow.

5. Never call your dog to you to correct him. He won't want to come when called because he thinks he may be in trouble. Always go to your Boxer to correct bad behavior, but be sure you catch him while he is doing something wrong, or he won't understand why he is in trouble.

6. Never, *ever* hit your dog as punishment. Nothing could be more damaging to your relationship with your Boxer than a physical correction. Hitting your dog will only make him afraid and distrustful of you, and he may react by growling or biting. Be sure to only use your voice to correct your Boxer, and keep your paws to yourself!

7. When you are rewarding your dog or correcting him, be sure to let your voice do the talking.

8. Use a light, happy voice when your Boxer does something good and a calm, firm voice when your dog does something wrong. Remember that your Boxer doesn't speak English any more than you speak German, but he can understand the tone of your voice.

meaning that they tend to look to the world around them, rather than their own-ers, for behavioral cues. It's natural, but it can be frustrating, especially when your Boxer questions your commands!

Organized obedience classes can help. They instruct you and your dog how to communicate with each other in a structured way that makes the training process easier. Trainers typically segregate their classes by age and ability: puppy kin-dergarten is for young pups, basic training is for the kindergarten graduates, and advanced obedience is for the experts. Go to the AKC's website to find obedience and puppy training classes in your area, at www.akc.org/events/trainingclubs.cfm.

Puppy Kindergarten

If your Boxer is a pup, the place to start is puppy kindergarten. Intended to be an opportunity for your puppy to socialize with other dogs and humans, this course introduces you and your Boxer to behavior basics, such as having the dog settle down on cue and look to you for guidance. It also teaches you how to be your dog's pack leader by asserting your dominance in a humane, loving way.
You can enroll your Boxer in puppy kindergarten when he is between eight and sixteen weeks old (but no older than twenty weeks). In most cases, your Boxer will have to complete at least two rounds of vaccinations to be allowed to enroll.

Basic Training Courses

After your Boxer graduates from kindergarten, you can take his training a step further by participating in basic and intermediate obedience training. If you have an adult Boxer that needs some training help, these courses are also open to older dogs.

Your Boxer will learn more specific cues, such as *sit, stay, leave it, take it, come, down,* and *heel.* You'll also get advice on how to handle problem behaviors,

Enroll your Boxer in training classes while he's young. Problem behavior from a puppy may be cute for a while but will grow tiresome as your Boxer reaches adulthood.

such as digging, barking, and chewing. These courses are for dogs that are four months of age or older.

Alternatively, you can also consider hiring a private trainer to come to your home. Normally reserved for dogs with severe behavior problems, private training is done one-on-one and can be individualized to fit you and your Boxer's needs and schedule.

Get Good Training Help

Here are suggestions for finding training professionals who are compatible with your philosophies and needs:

• Refer to the American Kennel Club's website (www.akc.org) for help finding obedience clubs and classes.

• Be clear about the kind of training you want for your dog. It helps to know this ahead of time, before you start shopping for trainers. Read training books and research online. Choose the philosophies that meet your needs.

• Locate trainers in your area. Look online and ask your dog-owning friends, veterinarian, and breeder for referrals. The Association of Pet Dog Trainers promotes dog-friendly training methods, and many of the organization's members are postive-method trainers. You can find a list of APDT member trainers in your area by searching their site, www.apdt.com.

• Interview potential trainers whom you're interested in. Be certain that their techniques, training methods, and services offered meet your training goals.

• Observe a class. Watch the trainer at work to be sure you are comfortable with the training methods and style.

• Ask for references. If a potential trainer says no to this request, then move on to someone else. Contact past students to find out about their experiences in class.

• Select the trainer you are most comfortable with, and sign up! Keep in mind that you can leave and go to another trainer at any time, if you become uncomfortable or disagree with anything the trainer does. Your Boxer's safety and well-being are the most important factors.

FINDING THE RIGHT TRAINER

Taking your Boxer to a puppy kindergarten or dog obedience class should be a fun and educational experience for both of you. It gives your pup a chance to socialize with other dogs and learn how to behave; and it gives you a chance to mingle with other dog owners—a bonus! You can usually find trainers who run these classes through your veterinarian's office, your local pet-supply store, online, or in the phone book.

Before you settle on a trainer, however, visit the class to observe the trainer in action and make sure you're comfortable with his or her training methods before enrolling. Here are some things you should look for when choosing a trainer and class for your Boxer:

- An interesting, enjoyable atmosphere
- Informative lessons
- Using positive-reinforcement training
- Ongoing education
- Vaccination requirements
- Positive references
- Satisfaction guarantee

Understanding Positive Reinforcement

Many different training theories and practices exist today. Trainers use different approaches to teach dogs how to behave. Some use a balanced method that incorporates positive reinforcement and correction. Others use a behavior-driven approach. Still others use tools, like clickers, to acknowledge a dog's proper behavior. One aspect that the successful and humane methods share is positive reinforcement.

Positive-reinforcement training utilizes treats, praise, and other behavior-driven techniques to encourage dogs to look to their owners for guidance on how to behave properly.

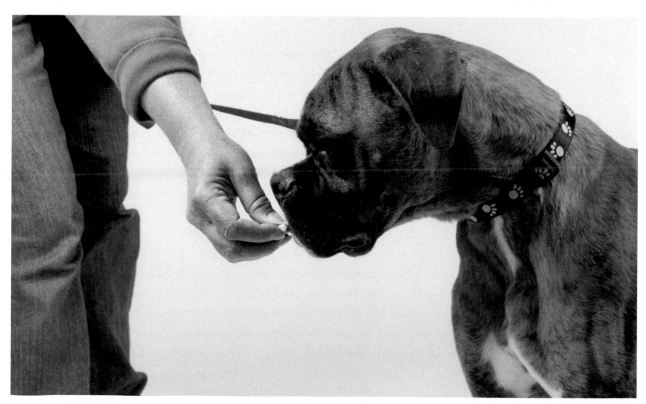

Puppy kindergarten and basic training classes will help your Boxer learn to properly interact with people and other dogs.

Positive reinforcement rewards obedient behavior with treats, praise, and lots of love. Timing is critical when using this approach. For example, when you're teaching your dog the basic *sit* cue, reward him immediately with a treat when he sits correctly. If he doesn't sit correctly, don't say "bad dog" and smack him with a rolled up newspaper. Instead, correct the behavior, gently showing him how to sit correctly, and then ask him to sit again. When he does sit, reward him with a treat and lots of praise.

Just as we are more inclined to repeat a behavior if we receive a positive response, the same is true for your Boxer. Dogs' behavior tells us that anything a dog does that is rewarded will be repeated. If something good happens when a dog does something (such as receiving a tasty treat or hugs and praise), he will want to do it again to get the reward again. So, be sure to have lots of dog treats in your pockets when training. The easiest way to let your pup know he did something right is to give him a treat!

Remember that your dog will respond to your verbal tones and their nuances. When the dog earns an upbeat "good boy" from his pack leader, he'll translate that as "I'm doing something my human likes." Alternatively, when the dog gets a gruff "no," he'll translate that as "Whoops. My human isn't happy. I shouldn't have done that." Your intonation and delivery communicate a great deal to your Boxer. Never shout or get angry at him; it will do more harm than good. Instead, use the same training idea—instead of giving a treat, use a cue word like "no" in a calm voice when prompting a correction to your dog's negative behavior and move him away from whatever he is doing wrong.

What is Clicker Training?

Treats can also be paired with a positive-reinforcement training technique called clicker training, which has gained mass popularity among dog trainers in recent years. Clicker training utilizes a small device that makes an audible "click" sound when pressed. Paired with treats at first, you "click" each time your puppy does something positive, such as obeying a cue or playing quietly on his own. After a few weeks, your puppy will begin to associate the clicking sound with the benefits of receiving treats and praise. Eventually, the sound of the clicker and a quick pat on the back will be reward enough for your Boxer to continue doing the proper behaviors you ask of him.

GETTING STARTED

Before you begin your training session, gather some treats, such as very small chunks of cooked chicken or cheese. Attach your Boxer's collar or harness to a 4-foot leash and lead him to an area where you'll have plenty of room to work. Plan to dedicate about 20 minutes a day to these training sessions, but practice the cues constantly in your day-to-day activities and encourage your family members to do the same.

Begin by teaching your Boxer to respond to his name when you say it. Stand in front of him, and say his name in a fun, upbeat voice. When he looks at you, reward him with lots of praise and a small piece of cheese or meat. Repeat this exercise often, until your Boxer appears to have caught on.

If he becomes distracted by a butterfly or a passing car, repeat his name and use a gentle nudge with your hand to remind him to look at you. His eyes should be on you whenever you say his name.

Practice this for a few days before you begin training, and soon, when your Boxer hears his name, he'll look at you and wait for something to happen.

Canine Good Citizen® Program

Most Boxers hone their service skills by participating in the American Kennel Club's Canine Good Citizen program.

Started in 1989, this AKC program recognizes dogs that demonstrate excellent manners at home and in the community. Often held in conjunction with or after puppy kindergarten and basic obedience training, the CGC program tests a dog's ability to pass a series of ten obedience tests, which are listed below. Dogs that pass, earn a certificate from the AKC and a dog tag inscribed with the title of "Canine Good Citizen."

To qualify to take the test, you must first sign the AKC's Responsible Dog Owners Pledge (see page 32), which affirms that you agree to care for your dog's health needs, safety, exercise, training, and quality of life. It also affirms that you agree to be responsible to the community by cleaning up after your dog and never letting him infringe on the rights of others.

After you sign the pledge, you're ready to start training to take the test. You'll need to outfit your dog with a well-fitting buckle or slip collar made of leather or fabric. The test facilitator will provide a 20-foot leash for the test.

To earn his CGC certificate, your Boxer has to successfully demonstrate the following ten test items.

Your Boxer's New Pack

Dogs are highly social creatures. This behavior traces back to their ancestors (wolves) that lived in closely knit packs with a social structure built around a dominance hierarchy. When dogs became part of human families, they viewed people as part of their pack structure and interacted with them using the same behavioral patterns they would for canine members of their pack.

Dogs happily accept a subordinate role to people. The degree to which they do depends on the dog's breed, gender, and individual differences. Females, for example, more readily accept dominance from humans than males.

Modern-day dogs love socialization, and they'll do almost anything for praise and affection—especially from a dominant member of their family! When you assert your role as pack leader early, you'll raise a healthy and well-integrated canine member of your family.

- **Accepting a friendly stranger:** Allow a friendly stranger to approach you and talk to you, while the dog is with you.

- **Sitting politely for petting:** Allow a friendly stranger to pet him while he's out with you or his handler.

- **Appearance and grooming:** Allow a stranger, such as a veterinarian or groomer, to examine and handle him. This test also demonstrates your dedication to your dog's care.

- **Out for a walk:** Showing that you (or his handler) are in control, the dog walks attentively beside you while you hold a loose leash and make right, left, and about turns.

- **Walking through a crowd:** Demonstrating the dog's ability to walk through a crowd of pedestrians.

- **Staying in place:** Showing that he obeys your *sit* and *stay* cues.

- **Coming when called:** Showing that he obeys your *come* cue.

- **Reacting to another dog:** Demonstrating that he behaves appropriately around other dogs.

- **Reaction to distraction:** Showing that he reacts confidently to distracting situations.

- **Supervised separation:** Demonstrating that he can be left alone with another person and maintain good manners.

Train your dog to respond to your training cues using small morsels of kibble or treats. Then enroll him in the AKC's Canine Good Citizen program to prove his merit.

You can find CGC training and testing programs through your kennel club, trainer, or some pet specialty stores. To learn more about the program, flip to page 76 and check out www.akc.org/events/cgc.

A play bow let's you know that your dog is in a good mood and ready to play with his favorite person—you!

Reading Your Boxer's Body Language

Dogs don't use words to communicate with humans, but they do use postures and body language to convey their moods. Canine body postures refer to the way a dog positions his body when he comes into contact with another dog or animal (including humans). It signals to the other animal whether he is feeling fearful, playful, submissive, or aggressive.

When you can identify these various postures, you can better understand your Boxer's behavior and mood, taking appropriate action when needed. Likewise, if another dog strikes an aggressive posture, you and your dog can walk away to prevent problems. Here are the common postures and their telltale signs.

• **Neutral relaxed:** When your Boxer is neutral relaxed, he's simply hanging out, enjoying the day. His head is erect, his ears are up, his tail is relaxed and wagging, his mouth is slightly open, and his weight is evenly distributed over all four feet.

• **Greeting:** Dogs that are saying hello to other dogs approach each other cautiously. The more dominant dog has his ears and tail up. The submissive dog has his ears back, tail down, and eyes semi-closed. The two sniff each other's genital regions. This may seem strange to humans, but it's completely natural to dogs. Dogs have glands on either side of the anus. These anal glands contain a scent that's unique to each dog. When they greet each other, dogs sniff at these glands as a way of learning who the other is. Talk about getting up close and personal!

• **Play bow:** When your Boxer wants to play, you'll know immediately when he strikes a play bow. He lowers his front end, including his head and shoulders, and leaves his hips high. He happily wags his tail with ears up, eyes soft, mouth relaxed, and tongue out. This posture lets everyone know that the dog is ready to play.

•   **Arousal:** A Boxer that has been stimulated by something—whether it be a sound, a sight, or a smell—will hold the arousal posture. The dog's ears are up and forward, his eyes are wide open, his tail is up, and his weight is over his front legs. His muzzle may appear tense, with his lips lifted to expose his teeth, and his hackles may be raised, especially if he's responding to an unfamiliar stimulus. If the dog is responding to something pleasurable, however, like when his best dog friend comes to the door, he wags his tail loosely and relaxes his muzzle, and his hackles are down. The dog knows something fun is about to happen, and he's ready for it.

•   **Defensive aggression:** If a dog feels threatened, he strikes a defensive-aggression posture, warning the other dog (or animal) that he doesn't want to be approached. His hackles may be up. His tail is down and tensed, and his ears are back. His weight falls over his rear legs. His muzzle is tense, and he may snarl and expose his teeth. A Boxer in this posture may attack or bite, if the offending animal doesn't back down.

•   **Aggressive attack:** A posture that no one likes to see, an aggressive attack pose, means your Boxer is in fight mode. It's a threatening posture intended to frighten, chase away, or attack intruders. Poorly socialized or highly protective Boxers may take this pose when they feel their home is being invaded or their human is threatened. When your dog is in this posture, you see a raised

When you see your dog's ears up and eyes wide open, he's attentive and focused on what's going on around him.

tail and hackles. His ears are erect, tilting forward, and his eyes shoot darts at his adversary. He curls his lips, revealing his teeth. His weight is on his front paws, and he'll likely be charging and barking.

● **Submission:** The opposite of aggression, submission is when a dog acknowledges the dominant animal by surrendering.

Behaviorists identify two types of submission:

1. **ACTIVE SUBMISSION:** The dog tilts his head down, lowers his tail, cocks his ears back, and half-closes his eyes. He may raise his paw, and his mouth may be partly closed with his tongue tip darting in and out.

2. **PASSIVE SUBMISSION:** The dog lays on his back, exposing his belly. He's essentially surrendering to the other animal. He cocks his ears back, turns his head away, and tucks his tail. This is the position your pup should take when you tell him to settle.

KEYS TO SUCCESSFUL TRAINING

During your Boxer's training, keep in mind that you need to be your dog's leader. Let him know that you are in charge. You'll have to teach him in a way that he will understand. Your puppy doesn't understand human rules, so be patient. It will take time for your Boxer to understand what you're trying to teach him—and for you to understand him. But your Boxer is intelligent, so it will happen. Above all else, throughout all of your training, remember to be patient, repeat lessons, keep the training sessions short and sweet, and always end on a positive note.

At a Glance ...

It's never too early to start your Boxer's obedience training. Puppies have a greater ability to retain new knowledge when they're young and impressionable.

· ·

After your pup has had all of his vaccinations and received a clean bill of health from your veterinarian, enroll him in a puppy kindergarten class to introduce him to other dogs his age and teach him how to interact appropriately with other dogs.

· ·

Positive-reinforcement training is by far the preferred method of most dog trainers today. Clicker training is a popular form of this training style.

· ·

After your Boxer has graduated from puppy kindergarten, consider enrolling him in the American Kennel Club's Canine Good Citizen® program. The program promotes positive social interactions for your dog within the community and is an important stepping-stone for further involvement in canine sporting and service opportunities.

· ·

Learn to read your dog's body language to determine his moods and to help you understand how he's trying to communicate with you. It can be invaluable during your training sessions, letting you know when your Boxer is paying attention, frustrated, or ready to move on from the lesson.

CHAPTER SIX

House-Training Your Boxer

House-training instructs your Boxer about when and where he can relieve himself. When you first bring him home, your puppy hasn't yet developed bladder control, and he won't be able to tell you that he needs to use the bathroom.

In time, however, your Boxer will learn to hold his bladder and bowels, let you know when he needs to go outside, and eliminate in a designated area. Until then, it's a game of watching

It will take some time for your Boxer to become fully house-trained. Puppies need six months or more to get used to the routine and holding their bladders.

your puppy's behavior for signs that he needs to go *before* he relieves himself all over the carpet.

You can train a puppy to eliminate where you want him to. For example, city dwellers often train their dogs to relive themselves at the curbside because large plots of grass are not readily available. Suburbanites, on the other hand, usually have yards to accommodate their dogs' needs.

The best time to start house-training is when your puppy is between seven and nine weeks old and his physical coordination has started to refine. Because your Boxer typically won't eliminate in the same space where he eats and sleeps, keeping your dog in his crate or in a restricted space during this time trains him to hold his bladder and bowels until it's time to visit the designated bathroom area.

Plan to continue house-training until your dog is six months old, and plan to limit his freedom throughout the house until he is a year old. By the end of this training period, you'll have confidence that your pup knows when and where to do his business. Each dog is different, but generally, Boxers can be house-trained by the time they are six to eight months old, as long as they're not required to hold it for too long. The process will take time. Be patient, stick to a schedule, and remember to praise your pup for doing the right thing!

A PIECE OF HISTORY

The first Boxer club was formed in Munich, Germany, in 1895. The club's founders wrote the first Boxer breed standard as a guide for future breeding, and much of that first standard still remains in the standard used today.

FOCUS ON THE POSITIVE

House-training can be stressful, so it's important to focus on the small victories and milestones along the way to successful training. First and foremost, the most effective way to train your Boxer is through positive reinforcement, which rewards good behavior with treats, praise, and lots of love.

When using positive reinforcement to house-train your Boxer, keep the following points in mind:

• **Reward your dog for doing the right thing.** Use positive motivators like treats, praise, and playtime, when your Boxer goes potty when and where you tell him to.

• **Correct him in the act and redirect his behavior.** When your Boxer makes a mistake (and he will!), correct him by saying "no" and then lead him to the correct bathroom area, praising him when he goes in the right spot.

• **Whatever you do, do it immediately.** Dogs have short memories. Whether you praise or correct your Boxer, he'll associate it with the act he just performed. Don't punish your dog after coming home from a long day of work to discover he's eliminated all over your kitchen. It won't do any good because your dog won't understand why you're so upset. Unless you catch your pup in the act or shortly thereafter, don't bother trying to correct the behavior. Wait until you catch the negative behavior, then redirect him to where you want him to go. You'll have a much higher success rate if you do.

Your Boxer simply wants to please you. When you reward his correct behavior with praise and love, he knows he did the right thing and will want to keep doing it to reap the rewards.

KEEP HIM CONTAINED

When your Boxer comes home, you probably won't know his house-training habits. He may have been living on sheets of newspaper and allowed to relieve himself anywhere he wanted, or he may understand the concept of going outside. Until you know his habits (and he learns how to control his bladder and bowels), you must limit his access to a certain area of the house.

You can restrict his freedom in several ways.

• **Using his crate**: Because your pup's instincts tell him not to eliminate where he eats and sleeps, you can use his crate to teach him bladder and bowel control. Limit his time in the crate to two hours at a time during the day, letting him periodically stretch his legs and play in his X-pen; at night, he'll stay in his crate until you let him out to go to the bathroom.

• **Using an X-pen**: These devices keep your Boxer contained in a small area that you can easily monitor. Because X-pens and playpens give your Boxer more space, your pup may choose a corner for a bathroom area. Line the entire surface with several layers of newspaper or some absorbent house-training pads to sop up accidents, and clean the area thoroughly if (and *when*) accidents happen.

Keep your Boxer safely contained in an X-pen or crate when you're unable to be home with him. But remember to let him out every few hours to go potty.

House-Training Tip

Be consistent. Always take your dog to the same location, always use the same command, and always have your dog on leash when he is in his bathroom area, unless a fenced-in yard is available.

By following the prescribed method, your puppy will be completely house-trained by the time his muscle and brain development reach maturity. Keep in mind that small breeds usually mature faster than large breeds, but all puppies should catch on to house-training by six months of age.

• **Giving your puppy supervised "freedom":** Of course you'll want to let your pup play while you're watching television or hanging out in the living room. It's perfectly fine to do this—as long as you (or a responsible family member) are there to keep a constant eye on him. Take your puppy outside to go to the bathroom regularly and lay down some absorbent pads, just in case.

As your Boxer becomes house-trained, you can slowly expand his area to include part of a room, then an entire room, and eventually the entire house. Your Boxer's successful potty-training hinges on you setting and following a bathroom schedule.

SETTING UP THE BATHROOM SPOT

Dogs are creatures of habit. House-training will be much easier for you and your Boxer if you designate a particular bathroom area and take your puppy there frequently throughout the day. When you're setting up your pup's potty spot, remember the following pointers.

• **Designate a space:** Choose a bathroom area outside and always take your pup on leash to that area. It could be a patch of grass or dirt, a curb, or even a litter box (albeit a large one) on your patio. Regardless of where you choose, always use the same spot.

• **Plan frequent visits to the bathroom area:** A young pup's bladder is tiny and doesn't hold much, so plan to take your Boxer outside frequently: after every meal, after playing, when waking up from one of his many naps, and about every half hour to two hours in between, depending on his development.

• **Go out with him:** You need to accompany your pup outside, using a cue word or phrase such as "go potty." Going with him is the only way to determine that he's going to the bathroom and not sniffing and playing instead. Eventually, your Boxer will be able to go on cue, which is very useful in the middle of the night or when you're traveling.

Your puppy may want to play when he goes outside, but cue him to go to the bathroom first. Doing so reinforces that he should do what you say first (take care of business) and then enjoy the reward of playing with you afterward.

• **Show your dog the other "living areas" in the home:** Besides learning where he *can* go to the bathroom, your Boxer also needs to learn where

Three Keys to House-Training

It's nice to have an obedient Boxer that will sit on cue or even down-stay off leash for sixty seconds, but it's not critical to your daily life. House-training, on the other hand, is critical, and it's at the top of the list of all behavior controls that an owner must accomplish. The most important aspects of successful house-training are:

1. CONSISTENCY—Your puppy is relying on you to establish a routine and stick to it. House-training is only important to you, not the puppy. If you want your puppy to succeed (and you definitely do!), then make a real effort to tackle this first training hurdle. Decide on a plan of action for how you want your dog to behave, then stick to it in your training.

2. REPETITION—Boxers are creatures of habit and need to understand what's expected of them. An owner can ingrain what is expected of his dog by repeating the same cues, and doing the same routine day after day until the puppy responds without failure.

3. WORD ASSOCIATION—Decide on the words you will use for house-training, and be consistent. "Go crate," "outside," and "go potty" are three of the most common phrases owners use to communicate with their dogs about when it's time to go.

he *can't* go to the bathroom. Aside from the frequented areas of your home, introduce your dog to other living areas, as well—like the bedrooms, guest room, dining room, and den. Once he recognizes these rooms as places where the family lives, he'll be less likely to use them as alternative bathroom spots.

• **Clean up accidents:** When your pup urinates or defecates someplace he shouldn't, clean up the mess with an enzyme-based cleanser and deodorizer. Dogs have a keen sense of smell; they'll sniff out a spot they've used before and return to use it again. Remove all traces of the accident so that he doesn't think it's another bathroom area.

GET INTO A ROUTINE

Teaching your puppy to go to the bathroom on cue and in the right place will challenge you both. Don't worry: it's not difficult. But everyone in your household must be committed to consistent training by following these same steps every time you take your Boxer to the bathroom. You can tweak the routine as your pup starts to get the hang of house-training.

Plan to follow this routine until your puppy is at least six months old, depending on your dog's maturity level. Even then, restrict his free access to the entire house until he's a year old. You want to be able to trust your Boxer completely, and even though six months or a year sounds like a long time, it's really not, when you compare it to a lifetime of no accidents!

Assuming that you've introduced your puppy to the entire house and his designated bathroom area, whether indoors or out, these step-by-step instructions can help guide you through the house-training process. Remember: follow these steps each and every time you take your pup to the bathroom.

1. When it's time to go outside, say "outside" in a happy, upbeat tone. Attach your Boxer's leash to his collar and lead him to the bathroom area. You'll want to let him do his business at regular times throughout the day, including:

• **Right when he wakes up in the morning and after every nap.** Puppy bladders won't hold much, and your Boxer will be ready to relieve himself after a full night's sleep or a relaxing nap. When your pup is very young, carry him to his bathroom area after he awakes; when he gets older and develops bladder control, you can walk him outside.

• **Right after he eats.** Most dogs need to do their business shortly after they eat. Take your puppy outside no more than fifteen minutes after he finishes his meal. Older dogs can wait a bit longer.

• **Right after he plays.** When puppies get excited, they sometimes lose control of their bladders. Right after a fun play session, take your pup to his designated bathroom area. As he gets

older and learns to control his bladder, you can eventually eliminate the need for this trip.

- **Right after you give him a bath.** That warm, sudsy water could trigger the urge to go potty, so take him outside as soon as he's bathed—and try to keep him out of the dirt!

- **Every two hours (or so).** At first, you'll take your pup outside every one to two hours to relieve himself (which includes the occasions listed above). Your Boxer will develop bladder and bowel control as he gets older, so you can adjust this rule as he matures.

- **Right before he goes to bed.** Take your puppy to the bathroom right before you put him in his crate at night, so that he makes it until morning.

2. **As soon as he starts going to the bathroom, say "go potty."** Your Boxer knows what he's doing, and giving him a verbal cue helps him mentally link his action with your cue. Teaching him to go on cue is particularly useful when it's raining or snowing outside, when you're late for work, or when you're on a road trip and don't have a lot of time to spare.

3. **Immediately after he's done, say "good job going potty" (or whatever phrase or word you choose) and give him a treat.** He'll begin to associate three things: the words ("go potty") with the action (going potty), the action with the reward (treat), and the reward with your praise. You're teaching him that by going potty on cue, he will earn a reward. That reward will ultimately be your praise.

Slowly, your Boxer will show signs of understanding the house-training concept. He'll begin to wait by the door when he has to go or come up with some other way to say, "I have to go to the bathroom now!" Eventually, he'll be able to

Take your dog to the same spot every time he goes to the bathroom. Eventually, he'll understand where he should go when he needs to go.

Home Cleaning Solutions

Your pup will inevitably have a few (or many!) accidents while house-training. Luckily, you can use many household items to help keep your home clean during this training stage.

■ If you don't have any professional cleaners on hand, create your own using ¼ cup of white vinegar to 1 quart of water.

■ Salt will absorb fresh urine and remove some of the scent.

■ In a pinch, rubbing the area with a dryer sheet can remove some of the odor.

■ White toothpaste can sometimes remove some tough stains from carpet. But beware—it can also ruin the carpet's coloring! Never use toothpaste on dark-colored carpets.

hold his bladder throughout the night without whimpering. Then he'll head to the bathroom area first thing when you let him outside. It will take time—at least six months—before he gets the hang of it, but rest assured that he will.

Prevention is key to house-training. Don't give your pup the opportunity to make a mistake. Keep him in your sight at all times by attaching his leash to your chair or waist, or using a baby gate to keep him confined. If you see him start to sniff around or walk in circles, immediately grab the lead and take him outside to his bathroom spot, saying "go potty." Then praise and give him a treat.

PAPER TRAINING

Typically used during the beginning stages of house-training, paper-training teaches your Boxer to eliminate on sheets of newspaper, rather than wherever he pleases. This method is useful when you can't supervise him or take him to his bathroom area during the day. It's also useful for pups that have developed a habit of going in their crates. However, it can be difficult to train your dog out of the habit of eliminating on papers indoors, if you eventually want to train him to go outside. If paper-training seems the most effective house-training tool for you, though, follow these simple steps.

1. Before your pup is allowed free reign of the house, erect an X-pen to confine him to one area. Choose a place such as the kitchen, living room, or other high-traffic area where he feels like he's part of the family pack.

2. Lay down three or four sheets of newspaper inside the entire pen. Your Boxer will develop a habit of eliminating on the newspaper, eventually preferring a specific spot to do his business.

3. Once your Boxer has chosen the spot where he prefers to eliminate and the rest of the papers remain clean, gradually reduce the area that is papered. Remove the sheets that are farthest away from his preferred spot. Eventually, you'll only need to leave a few sheets in the designated area.

4. After your pup is reliably going on the papers that you've left, slowly start to move the paper to a location that's more to your liking (that is to say, not in the middle of the floor or under the kitchen table). Don't move the papers too far too soon: an inch or two a day is far enough.

Don't be discouraged if your pup misses the paper or makes remarkable progress and then regresses. Lay down a larger area of newspaper and start again. It's normal to make mistakes. Just stay determined, and your Boxer will eventually get the hang of it.

ACCIDENT CLEANUP

You've been taking your Boxer puppy to his bathroom area regularly and letting him relieve himself after every meal, playtime, and nap. Your dog is slowly becoming house-trained. But then he makes a mistake. What do you do?

The act of going to the bathroom isn't the mistake; going in the wrong place is the problem. So if you catch your pup in the act, say "no" in a corrective tone and immediately take him to his bathroom area and let him finish his business there. Then praise your Boxer and celebrate that he is going outside.

Clean the soiled area with white vinegar or an enzymatic pet-stain cleaner. Dogs tend to continue soiling in areas that smell like feces or urine, so removing all traces of the accident will prevent your Boxer from using that area again.

Don't correct your dog after he makes a mistake; he can't understand the connection between the correction and the mistake he made hours (even minutes) ago. And never, *ever* rub your dog's face in the mess. Not only is it an unnecessarily harsh punishment, but your dog will think that you are mad because he defecated, not because he went in the wrong place. Instead, encourage and praise your dog even more when he does go in his correct bathroom area.

It's also important to keep a close eye on your Boxer. If you know where your dog is, he can't make a mistake. A circling and sniffing dog means he's searching for a bathroom, so ask him in an upbeat happy voice, "Do you have to go potty?" When he runs to the door, take him out and praise him after he goes.

At a Glance ...

The keys to successful house-training are consistency, patience, and positive reinforcement.

Start your puppy's house-training ASAP—from the moment you bring your Boxer home, teach him the appropriate place to go to the bathroom.

Use the same cue words and follow the same route to the potty spot every time your puppy needs to go. It will help ingrain the training in your pup's mind and prepare him to alert you every time he needs to go to the bathroom.

Paper-training can be a great help to for owners who don't have easy access to an outside bathroom area for their dogs or who aren't home often enough throughout the day to take their puppies out. However, keep in mind that it can be confusing for the dog to learn when it's appropriate to go outside or inside on the paper.

Don't punish your pup when he has an accident in the house. Instead, take him to the correct potty spot to finish, and praise him for a job well done. Dogs have a short attention span, so if you don't catch your Boxer in the act, he won't understand what behavior you're trying to correct.

CHAPTER SEVEN

Training and Conditioning

If you want everyone to love your Boxer as much as you do, you need to teach your dog good manners. In the canine world, that means things like coming, sitting, staying, and heeling whenever you ask. Puppyhood is the best time to begin teaching your Boxer. Puppies are like sponges; they are ready to absorb all that you can teach them. So, the earlier you start training, the easier it will be.

Every Boxer should grow up to be able to pass the American Kennel Club's Canine Good

Dogs Will Be Dogs

Although more people these days tend to think of their dogs as their "children," it's important to remember that dogs are dogs, and they need to be treated as such. Treating your pet like a miniature human will only confuse him. He wants to be part of the pack, not your youngest child.

Citizen test, which is an indication that he is a well-behaved canine member of society. All dog owners benefit from other owners taking responsibility for their dogs' manners and obedience training. A dog that can sit, stay, heel, and come on call will be welcomed and admired wherever he goes.

TEACH SETTLE

The *settle* cue shows your Boxer that you are the alpha dog. It teaches him that when you say "settle," it means he needs to calm down and submit to you.

Here's an easy way to teach this cue to your Boxer puppy:

1. Sit in a chair or on the floor, and flip your dog over in your lap so his belly is up, putting him in a submissive position.

2. Calmly say "settle."

3. When he relaxes in your arms, say "good boy to settle" and give him a treat.

If your dog refuses to settle, use a more direct voice while gently touching his throat area, similar to the behavior a mother dog would use with a misbehaving puppy. Because the throat is a dog's most vulnerable area, he'll instinctively respond.

This cue is very useful when your Boxer decides to tear around the house or misbehaves uncontrollably. Simply pick up your dog and say "settle." When he calms down, reward him with praise and set him free again.

As your Boxer grows, you obviously won't be able to scoop him up in your arms and tell him to settle. You can, however, train him to lie on his back in a submissive posture and show you his belly.

TEACH SIT

The *sit* cue teaches your dog to hold still in a seated position. A very important lesson in self-control, this cue is likely the first one your Boxer will learn, and it's the cornerstone of more training to come.

The easiest way to teach this cue is to use a treat as a lure. Follow these steps:

1. Stand in front of your dog. Bend down and hold a treat over his nose.

2. In a firm voice, say "sit." As you say the word, move the treat up over his head toward his tail. Your dog will follow the treat with his eyes and head, which will cause his rear to lower to a seated position. If he doesn't sit, show him what you want him to do by gently pushing his rear end down, while saying "sit."

3. Praise your dog when he does as he's asked (whether on his own or with a little help from you). Say "good dog" and reward him immediately with a treat.

Do this repeatedly until your Boxer understands that his obedience brings a reward—and your praise.

TEACH DOWN

The *down* cue teaches your Boxer to lie down and remain in place. You can use this cue for anything ranging from when you want your Boxer to lie down on his bed and play with a toy or to stay away from the table when you and your family are eating.

1. Begin by telling your dog to sit.

2. Holding a treat in front of his nose, say "down" and move the treat toward the floor in front of your dog's paws. As his nose follows the treat, he will lie down.

3. Praise your Boxer and give him the treat.

Repeat this process until he has mastery of the *down* cue down.

TEACH STAY

The *stay* command, used with both the *sit* and *down* cues, trains your Boxer to remain in place until you release him. The *sit-stay* cue is for shorter periods of time; the *down-stay* is for longer periods. Here's how to teach your Boxer the *stay* cue:

1. Start by facing your dog and telling him to sit.

2. With an open palm facing his nose, say "stay."

3. Slowly take one step backward and stay there.

4. If your Boxer stays in place, go back to him after a few seconds and reward him with treats and praise. If your dog fidgets and moves toward you, enlist the help of a friend or relative. Have your helper hold your Boxer's leash gently

Did You Know?

Many Boxers have great success in performance events, from obedience to rally to agility and more. However, the same intelligence that makes him a quick learner can lead to some frustration. The Boxer certainly has a mind of his own. You may find that your dog will invent the most unexpected games throughout his training and show performance.

but firmly after you give the cue. Repeat the process until your Boxer is trained and stays in place for long periods of time. Be sure to heap plenty of praise on your pup throughout these lessons.

5. Gradually increase the time your Boxer must stay put, as well as your distance from him, as he gets the hang of this cue.

TEACH COME

After *stay*, teach your Boxer the *come* cue, which is one of the most important cues to master. Your Boxer must learn to come to you immediately the first time you call him. Learning to obey this cue will keep your dog out of danger. Luckily, this cue is easy to teach. Here's how:

1. Start with your Boxer on a fairly short leash. Ask him to sit and stay.

2. Using a treat as a lure, say "come" and walk backward. Your dog will most likely follow you.

3. Reward and praise him when he reaches you.

Continue doing this with gradually longer leashes, even up to 20 feet long. Soon, your dog will run right to you every time you call him to come, which is exactly what you want.

Never call your dog to come to you for a correction or to scold him. That will quickly teach him to run away when you use the cue! Dogs think in the present tense, and your dog will connect the scolding with the act of coming to you, rather than the misbehavior from a few moments earlier.

TEACH HEEL

Teaching your dog to heel will make walking him on a leash a more fun and enjoyable experience for both of you.

Here's how to teach your dog the *heel* cue:

1. Connect the leash to your Boxer's collar or harness. Hold the leash with both hands, putting your right hand through the loop and holding the leash with your left.

2. With your dog on your left side, bend down and show the dog the treats in your right hand.

3. Move the treat slowly in front of him as if you're leading him by the nose, backing up.

4. Continue walking backward, all the while holding the treat where your dog can see it. As he follows you, praise and reward him.

5. When your Boxer follows you effortlessly, turn so that you and your dog are walking side-by-side, with your dog on your left side.

6. Continue to increase the length of your stroll until your dog walks beside you without pulling.

If your Boxer decides that he's going to walk (or pull) *you*, simply put on the brakes. Stand your ground until your dog realizes that he is not going anywhere until he walks beside you at your chosen pace. It may take some time to convince your Boxer that you are leading the walk, but be patient, rewarding and encouraging him when he does submit to you. Eventually, he'll catch on.

BOXERS BEHAVING BADLY

To be a well-mannered and obedient dog, your Boxer will need to follow your rules for the household. Occasionally, however, problems can occur, especially when your Boxer is a puppy.

Some of the behaviors that we perceive as "problems" are natural to dogs. Barking, for example, is how dogs communicate. Chewing relieves discomfort when their baby teeth fall out. These are normal dog behaviors. But when temporary behaviors become habits or when they're done inappropriately—like relentlessly barking or chewing your antique dresser—the action needs to be corrected.

The same positive-reinforcement training you used to teach your Boxer basic cues, such as *sit* and *stay*,

Be Safe and Be Happy

The *leave it* cue is important for letting a dog know who is the leader, as well as for his safety. Dogs, especially puppies, like to explore the world with their mouths. But that can be very dangerous.

If you are walking your dog and you come across a dead bird or a discarded piece of food, the last thing you want is for your Boxer to put it in his mouth! That could make him very sick. You want to quickly say "leave it" and know your dog will respond.

A Boxer that will leave it on cue is a Boxer likely to live a healthy life—and have a better taste in his mouth!

Can Your Dog Pass the Canine Good Citizen® Test?

An AMERICAN KENNEL CLUB Program

Once your Boxer is ready for advanced training, you can start training him for the American Kennel Club Canine Good Citizen® program. This program is for dogs that are trained to behave at home, out in the neighborhood, and in the city. It's easy and fun to do. Once your dog learns basic obedience and good canine manners, a CGC evaluator gives your dog ten basic tests. If he passes, he's awarded a Canine Good Citizen® certificate. Many trainers offer classes with the test as the final "graduation" class. To find an evaluator in your area, go to www.akc.org/events/cgc/cgc_bystate.cfm.

Many therapy dogs and guide dogs are required to pass the Canine Good Citizen® test in order to help as working dogs in the community. There are ten specific tests that a dog must pass in order to pass the Canine Good Citizen® test. A well-trained dog will:

1. Let a friendly stranger approach and talk to his owner.
2. Let a friendly stranger pet him.
3. Be comfortable being groomed and examined by a friendly stranger.
4. Walk on a leash and show that he is in control and not overly excited.
5. Move through a crowd politely and confidently.
6. Sit and stay on command.
7. Come when called.
8. Behave calmly around another dog.
9. Not bark at or react to a surprise distraction.
10. Show that he can be left with a trusted person away from his owner.

In order to help your dog pass the AKC CGC test, first enroll him in a series of basic training classes and CGC training classes. You can find classes and trainers near you by searching the AKC website. When you feel that your Boxer is ready to take the test, locate an AKC-approved CGC evaluator to set up a test date, or sign up for a test that is held at a local AKC dog show or training class. For more information about the AKC Canine Good Citizen® program, visit the website at www.akc.org/events.cgc.

will apply to corrective training, too. You need to correct the bad behavior and reinforce the good behavior. You can do this in several ways, depending on the particular action that you're trying to correct. No matter how frustrated you get with your Boxer's negative action, remember you have a variety of tools at your disposal to help redirect his behavior.

• **Voice:** The tone of your voice communicates emotion or feeling to your dog. An upbeat, higher-pitched tone communicates happiness or excitement. A lower-pitched, guttural tone communicates anger or sternness. Your Boxer will respond to these sounds as he would to his mother or pack leader's yelp or growl.

• **Consistency:** Be consistent in your corrective training. Stick to your guns and hold others to the training, too. For instance, if your Boxer is not allowed to receive table scraps from you, make sure your visitors know it as well. When everyone who comes into contact with your Boxer requires the same behavior from him, he won't get confused.

• **Correction, not punishment:** Correction should never, *ever* include physical punishment. Hitting, shocking, or harming your Boxer in any way can create an animal that fears people. Correction, instead, involves getting your Boxer's attention and stopping the behavior at that moment.

Before you begin corrective training, check with your veterinarian. Some bad behavior, such as chronic house-soiling or chewing, can be caused by medical conditions. Other troublesome behaviors can be exacerbated by your dog's diet or lack of exercise. Make sure your Boxer receives a clean bill of health from his vet, and then begin your training.

Use the tone of your voice to help you better communicate with your dog. A high-pitched tone says you're happy, while a low tone conveys disapproval—similar to the verbal communication among dogs.

Practice Makes Perfect

Like any other skill, your Boxer's obedience training will only get better with practice. Here are some tips to make it easier:

• **Keep it short:** Have training lessons with your dog every day in several short segments—three to five times a day for a few minutes at a time is ideal. Avoid long practice sessions; your dog will bore easily and stop paying attention.

• **Stay focused:** Never train when you're tired, sick, worried, or in an otherwise bad mood. Dogs sense our moods, and your Boxer will respond to a negative mood with poor performance.

• **Make it fun!** When you're training your pup, make the lessons fun, short, and positive. Rather than ending with a failed exercise, end on a high note with a training cue that your Boxer has mastered and follow this with lots of verbal praise. Enjoy the training, and your Boxer will enjoy it, too!

Quell Barking

Dogs bark to communicate. From protecting their homes from strangers to trying to get your attention, barking is a natural dog behavior. Guarding the home can be a positive reason to bark, and it's likely that your Boxer will vocalize only when he feels that he needs to. Before you begin corrective training, you need to determine why your dog is barking. Ask yourself:

• **Do you react to him every time he barks?** If so, then your Boxer has trained you! He knows that he'll get your attention if he barks.

• **Does he bark when someone comes to the door?** If so, he's protecting his territory.

• **Does he bark when nobody's home?** He may be suffering from separation anxiety.

After you've narrowed down some reasons why your dog barks, you can start correcting his behavior.

When your dog barks, don't yell at him. To your Boxer, yelling sounds like barking, and he'll think that you're telling him something! Instead, ignore the

Stopping Separation Anxiety

A dog with separation anxiety exhibits extreme behavior problems when left alone. After his owner leaves, the dog exhibits a panic response and will dig, chew, or scratch at the door trying to get to his owner. He will howl, cry, and bark, and may even urinate or defecate from distress.

Some things seem to trigger separation anxiety. Dogs that are used to constantly being with their owners but are suddenly left alone for the first time may exhibit panicky behavior. A traumatic event, such as time spent in a shelter or kennel, may trigger the anxiety. A change in the family's routine or structure, such as a child leaving for college, can also cause stress in the dog's life.

If you believe your Boxer is suffering from separation anxiety, here are some ways to correct the behavior:

• Keep your departures and arrivals low key. Quietly leave the house, and ignore your dog for a few minutes before acknowledging him when you return.

• Leave your dog with an item of clothing that smells like you.

• If your dog chews excessively when you are gone, leave him with a chew toy filled with treats.

More severe cases of separation anxiety require you to systematically train your dog to get used to being alone. Discuss options with your veterinarian and trainer—they may be able to offer more long-term solutions, such as prescription drugs for separation anxiety that can be used during behavior-modification training.

barking. This may sound difficult, but if your dog realizes that he won't get any attention when he barks, he's more likely to stop the behavior. Reward him for not barking by saying "good dog for being quiet" in an upbeat voice.

Enlist a friend to come to your door and ring the doorbell. Wait until your Boxer stops barking, say "good quiet" and reinforce the quiet behavior by praising and treating your dog. Your Boxer will soon learn that staying quiet will earn him praise.

If your Boxer is a stubborn barker, try the "shake-the-can" method. Place a dozen pennies in an empty aluminum can and tape it closed. When your dog barks, give the can a quick shake and say "quiet." The noise will distract the pup, startling him into silence. When he understands the consequences of barking (the loud rattling) and associates your correction with the noise, you can start using just the *quiet* cue.

Prevent Biting

Mouthing is normal behavior in puppies. Between four to twelve weeks old, your dog learns bite inhibition from his mother and littermates. He learns the amount of mouth pressure he can use without causing pain or harm when playing with his brothers and sisters. He tests how hard he can bite them without causing them to squeal. If he is removed from his littermates before learning this inhibition, it is up to you to teach him.

Teach your dog to stay on your cue. It will help you better control his behavior, which is safer for all.

It's best to train your Boxer never to bare his teeth (touch his teeth to skin or clothing) or bite. This is one of the most important lessons you can teach your dog. Start your "no-bite" training as soon as possible to ensure your dog's mouthing habit doesn't develop into something dangerous. Your Boxer should know not to bite by the time he is eighteen weeks old.

When your puppy nips or bites you, or even just mouths you, say "no bite." If he bites you, stop playing with him and walk away. Don't allow your dog to nip at your heels or chase your feet, either. He must learn that biting and nipping result in withdrawal of your attention.

If your Boxer continues to use his mouth and bite, even after your consistent training, discuss the situation with your veterinarian, who may be able to recommend a professional trainer or animal behaviorist to help you deal with the problem.

Redirect Chewing

Chewing, like digging or barking, is something dogs naturally do. Between three and six months of age, puppies begin to teethe, and with teething comes chewing—and puppies will chew anything and everything. As a puppy's baby teeth fall out and the adult teeth grown in, chewing relieves the discomfort, just as it does for human babies. Puppies go through a second chewing phase when they're between seven and nine months old, as part of exploring their territory.

Unfortunately, puppies develop a fondness for chewing during these phases. It relieves tension and anxiety, and it makes their sore gums feel better. For adult dogs, chewing massages their gums, removes plaque buildup on the teeth, and occupies their time. Chewing the wrong things, however, can be destructive to your home and dangerous to your Boxer's digestive tract.

In anticipation of your puppy's inevitable chewing, provide him with his own chew toys early on. Make sure they're size-appropriate toys, such as hard rubber balls stuffed with treats, nylon bones, or rope tug toys. And limit your puppy's toys to a few; you don't want your Boxer to think everything is available for his chewing pleasure!

No Jumping Up!

In Boxer language, jumping up means "I'm a happy dog" and "pay attention to me!" By jumping up, your dog shows that he wants to be the center of attention. Unfortunately, an exuberant Boxer could knock over a houseguest, so it's best to prohibit this behavior.

It's imperative not to acknowledge your dog's cries for attention when he jumps up. Don't pet him or pick him up, as tempting as it may be! Instead, tell your Boxer to sit. Only pet him after he obeys. Eventually, he'll learn that if he wants attention, he'll have to sit—not jump up.

Your Boxer also needs to learn to sit for other people. Use the leash if you must, and when your guests come to the door and your Boxer jumps up, say "no jumping," followed by "sit." Tell your guests that they're free to praise and give your dog the attention he wants after he sits for a period of time.

Everyone in your home must practice this correction early and consistently, if you hope to see results. Your Boxer needs to learn that the only way he'll get attention is if he sits first. Praise your dog lavishly every time he behaves correctly. Soon, your pup will know to sit before every greeting.

What About the Frenzies?

There will be times when your Boxer puppy will suddenly dash around your house or yard for no reason, seeming to flee from some unseen hunter. He's clearly burning off some pent-up energy, but is it normal? Totally.

These frenzies, or quick energy bursts are usually followed by an extra-long nap. The only thing you need to worry about is your pup crashing into something, hurting himself or injuring someone else.

Be a proud Boxer owner and show off your well-trained, well-behaved dog. With proper training, your Boxer will be the talk of the town!

Training Equipment

Before you begin training your Boxer, arm yourself with appropriate training equipment, including a training collar, a leash, treats, and (if you choose) a clicker.

• **Collar:** Different from his everyday collar, your Boxer's training collar should be light and flexible, yet strong enough to control the dog. Nylon collars work particularly well for training.

• **Leash:** In most cases, you'll use a 4- or 6-foot leash for training your Boxer. You may also choose to invest in a longer 20-foot leash for teaching your dog to come. As with the collar, a lightweight, flexible leash made of nylon works well for training purposes.

• **Treats:** Treats—more specifically, food rewards—are the ultimate motivator for training dogs because they teach the dog to associate proper behavior with a reward. Eventually, your verbal acknowledgement will be enough of a reward, but until your Boxer learns the association between your praise and his actions, you need to have a bag of treats on hand. Choose nutritious goodies, like small chunks of cooked chicken or squares of cheese, rather than things like processed hot dogs or dried biscuits.

• **Clicker:** Clickers are another way to associate good behavior with a reward. When your Boxer does something correctly, mark it by using a clicker (a mechanical device that makes a clicking sound). At first, you'll issue a click with a food reward. Eventually, the treat won't be needed, and the click and verbal praise will suffice.

• **Safety:** If you're
outside and your dog
starts to chase a bird,
you want him to be well
trained so he comes
back and stays at your
command. The untrained
Boxer will keep running
and can hurt himself,
lose his way home, or
worse.

• **Manners:** A well-
behaved Boxer will sit
and lie down quietly at
your side without bark-
ing, nipping, or trying to
run away.

• **Harmony:** A well-
behaved dog will be a
pleasure to be around.
If he starts to act ram-
bunctious, he'll settle
when told, or he'll lie
down in his bed when
you want to relax and
enjoy a movie.

As your pup ages, these races will wane. But until then, keep an eye on him when he runs around like a little maniac, and make sure he does not attempt to snap or grab at things as he bolts through the house. You do not want to prompt him to snatch at moving things because this could lead to chasing and biting at joggers and bicyclists.

Professional Help

Sometimes your Boxer's bad habits are just too much for you to handle. You've tried positive reinforcement. You've tried corrective approaches. But your Boxer still won't stop barking or jumping up on your houseguests. The most effective way to get your misbehaving Boxer back on track is to enlist the help of a profes-sional dog trainer.

You can find a professional dog trainer through referrals from your veterinarian, breeder, or local Boxer club. You can also find them through organizations, such as the Association of Pet Dog Trainers (www.apdt.com) or the Certification Council for Professional Dog Trainers (www.ccpdt.org) that allow you to search for trainers by location.

To ensure that you and your dog will get the best possible training, select a trainer who has been certified by the CCPDT. To earn the certification, trainers must demonstrate their dog-training knowledge and experience, and they must continue to educate themselves about the latest in training techniques and equipment.

FURTHER TRAINING

All of the basic cues outlined in this chapter are taught in puppy kindergarten training classes. To find an obedience class in your area, check with your veterinarian, breeder, local pet store, or breed club. Keep in mind that the more knowledgeable you are about your dog's training, the more successful he will be. Enforce these basic cues and anything else taught in the class by making them a part of your Boxer's daily routine.

If your dog takes well to his training, there are endless ways to use it beyond merely in the home and around your neighborhood. First, look into enrolling your pup in the AKC S.T.A.R. Puppy Program (see page 48), which will give your puppy a great foundation as a valued family companion. To find out more, visit www.akc.org/starpuppy. You can also search for a trainer who teaches the AKC's Canine Good Citizen program (see page 76), which encourages responsible pet ownership and rewards dogs with good manners. More information is available at www.akc.org/events/cgc/index.cfm. From there, it's on to service or therapy work, or a variety of canine sports ranging from obedience and conformation (dog shows) to agility and rally. The AKC offers events in all of these sports, which we'll discuss more in-depth in chapter 11.

Well-trained Boxers can participate in a variety of activities in the community, such as serving as therapy dogs or competing in canine sports.

At a Glance ...

A well-trained dog is a pleasure to be around. Don't neglect your Boxer puppy's training and let him grow up to be an unruly adult with no regard for authority. Begin obedience training early, while he's still an impressionable puppy.

. . . .

Basic obedience training teaches the dog important behaviors like sit, stay, down, heel, and come. All these and more are taught in puppy kindergarten classes, obedience classes, or private in-home training.

. . . .

The American Kennel Club's S.T.A.R. Puppy and Canine Good Citizen programs can help your Boxer to become a well-mannered, stellar canine member of society.

. . . .

Basic obedience lays the groundwork for many great activities that your Boxer can participate in outside of the home, such as service or therapy work and a variety of AKC sports including conformation (dog shows), agility, and rally.

CHAPTER EIGHT

Notes on Nutrition

Feeding dogs is different from feeding people, or it should be! We regularly eat unbalanced diets—skipping meals, snacking excessively, and overeating late at night. But it's important to set a better example for our pets. Dogs require more structure, and they need high-quality, nutritious food in the right amounts on a regular schedule. Major dog food manufacturers offer foods for dogs of every size, age, and activity level.

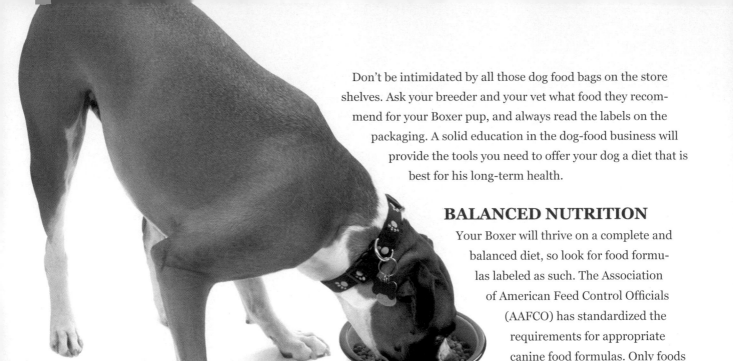

Don't be intimidated by all those dog food bags on the store shelves. Ask your breeder and your vet what food they recommend for your Boxer pup, and always read the labels on the packaging. A solid education in the dog-food business will provide the tools you need to offer your dog a diet that is best for his long-term health.

BALANCED NUTRITION

Your Boxer will thrive on a complete and balanced diet, so look for food formulas labeled as such. The Association of American Feed Control Officials (AAFCO) has standardized the requirements for appropriate canine food formulas. Only foods with approval from the AAFCO are allowed to use the "complete and balanced" label, meaning they meet the nutritional standards for dogs at their various stages of life. Manufacturers earn this label either by conducting strictly controlled feeding trials or by matching their products to a detailed nutrient profile.

A complete and balanced diet contains all the proper nutrients needed to keep your Boxer growing and in good health. Your dog's size and activity level will determine the amount of food he will need each day. Give him the amount of food suggested on the packaging at first, then keep an eye on his waist. Adjust his portions as necessary, and ask your veterinarian for advice if you have any questions or concerns.

Like us, dogs need a combination of carbohydrates, proteins, fats, vitamins, and minerals in their daily diets to stay healthy. The correct percentage of each of these nutrients changes as your dog ages, but the basic ingredients remain the same throughout your dog's life.

Clamoring for Kibble

It may not look too appetizing to humans, but kibble (dry food) tastes delicious to dogs. The kibble's shape, size, texture, smell, and taste have been researched and tested by scientists and veterinary nutritionists, who develop recipes, conduct feeding trials, and check for complete nutrition to ensure that dry food meets the U.S. Food and Drug Administration's and AAFCO's standards.

Kibble has some definite advantages. Boxers digest dry food easily. Made by cooking the ingredients together in big batches that are then cut into kibble-size bites and baked, dry food is often the least expensive food option. Because it is baked, dry food does not spoil quickly. Plus the kibble's crunch helps prevent plaque and tartar from forming on your dog's teeth. You can add variety to your Boxer's dry-food diet by feeding semi-moist or canned food periodically or by offering a mix of wet and dry food at mealtimes.

Changing Diets

When you bring home your new Boxer, be careful about changing to a completely different dog food right away. That quick change could make your dog sick. If you plan to switch from the food fed by his breeder, take home a small supply of the breeder's food to mix with your own. Make the change slowly to aid your puppy's adjustment to his new food.

Dry food may pose a challenge for Boxers with dental problems or those recovering from surgery because they can't bite into or digest the hard pieces of food. Sometimes the dried morsels aren't appealing enough for a picky dog's discriminating taste. Most breeders recommend kibble mixed with warm water and a little canned food.

Sweet on Semi-Moist

Semi-moist foods have a clay-like texture and are soft to the bite. They come in all shapes and sizes, from bite-size morsels and patties to whimsical shapes that look more like treats than food. They often come in resealable bags to lock in the moisture. Also formulated to serve the nutritional needs of the dog, semi-moist food contains more water than kibble, which makes it easier to chew for elderly dogs or those with dental problems. The food also smells more appetizing to finicky dogs.

To give the semi-moist food its look and texture, however, manufacturers often add chemicals, artificial sweeteners, and colors. Read the label and check the food's nutritional content before feeding it to your Boxer. A high amount of corn syrup or artificial sweetener can affect your dog's metabolism, causing him to gain weight. It can also lead to plaque and tartar buildup on your dog's teeth, which could result in gum disease.

Stew-Like Goodness

Big chunks of meat in hearty, rich gravy look delicious to dogs. Available in countless flavors, combinations, and recipes, canned foods combine the protein, carbohydrates, fats, and water in a way that caters to many dogs' taste buds. It may not smell good to humans, but most dogs love it.

Canned food has a high water content—up to 70 percent water, by weight—which supplies the Boxer with much-needed fluids. Its taste attracts picky eaters, it's easier than kibble for the dog to bite and chew, and it comes in perfectly packaged quantities for bigger diets. Canned food has a long shelf life and works well for dogs traveling to shows or obedience trials.

However, canned food generally costs more. It will spoil if left out for too long, and leftovers must be refrigerated. Some Boxer owners worry about what animal parts are used in canned foods, as well as the additives and preservatives that contribute to that long shelf life. Also, it can cause diarrhea in some dogs and can cause tartar and plaque to build up on their teeth. Again, read the label and consult with your veterinarian.

A PIECE OF HISTORY

Although the first Boxer to finish an AKC championship was in 1915 (a male named Sieger Dampf v Dom, owned by Boxer fanciers Governor and Mrs. Lehman of New York), there were few females in America for breeding, and the dog had no lasting influence on the breed. It wasn't until the early 1930s that Boxer popularity—and breeding programs—grew in the U.S.

Price Does Matter

You get what you pay for when it comes to dog food; but don't presume expensive is automatically better. Generally, the ingredients used in premium brands are higher-grade, come from whole-food sources, and contain fewer fillers than the less-expensive labels. They frequently contain added nutrients, too, such as antioxidants and vitamin supplements, which benefit senior dogs, overweight dogs, or specific breeds like your Boxer.

Some formulas that are less expensive use grains and other plant proteins for bulk. Though attractively priced, these diets may not satisfy your Boxer like food based on animal proteins. Many grain-based diets rely on soy protein, which can cause uncomfortable gas issues.

When in doubt, your veterinarian can help you choose a diet that's right for your dog.

Potentially Poisonous Foods

- Alcoholic beverages
- Apple seeds
- Apricot pits
- Bread dough
- Cherry pits
- Chocolate
- Candy or cookies containing the artificial sweetener xylitol
- Coffee (this includes coffee grounds, coffee beans, and coffee-flavored candy)
- Grapes and raisins
- Hops
- Macadamia nuts
- Mushroom plants
- Mustard seeds
- Onions and onion powder
- Peach pits
- Potato leaves
- Rhubarb leaves
- Salt
- Tea
- Tomato leaves and stems
- Walnuts

Alternative Diets Abound

Although commercial diets contain everything a dog needs to thrive, some people prefer to prepare their dogs' meals themselves. Raw and homemade diets allow Boxer owners to have more control over what they feed their pets.

Raw Food: There are varying opinions on raw diets, which consist of raw meat and bones that you feed to your dog. Some believe a raw diet improves dogs' skin, coat, and teeth, and increases their stamina and vitality. Others caution against E. coli, parasites, and other risks associated with raw meats. These diets must be supplemented by some source of fiber and vitamins to ensure the full range of nutrients.

Some pet stores sell raw diets. Often found in freezers, these foods are individually packaged to make feeding simple.

Homemade Food: Homemade diets are meals made from scratch. Often fed to finicky dogs or those with food allergies and similar to food made for humans, these diets incorporate whole foods, such as potatoes or rice, and protein sources, such as cooked chicken or beef, that aren't packed full of preservatives. Boxers eat a lot, so preparing homemade meals can be time consuming, but you can make these meals in larger quantities and freeze or refrigerate them. Be sure that you include all the nutrients that your Boxer needs.

Your Boxer will tolerate diet changes, but to protect his health, consult your veterinarian before introducing your dog to a raw or homemade diet. You can also consult a board-certified veterinary nutritionist to help you develop a diet for your Boxer. You may even want to talk to a holistic veterinarian to hear more opinions.

WATER, WATER EVERYWHERE!

Protein, carbohydrates, fats, vitamins, and minerals may be important to eat, but your Boxer needs to drink, too! Like humans, dogs' bodies require plenty of hydration to function normally. Water keeps their digestive systems working, their mucus membranes lubricated, and their cells replicating. It flushes their systems and keeps their bodies free from harmful toxins. Dogs need water to live.

With normal play and exercise, your pup will need to replenish his water supply frequently. On hot days or after exuberant exercise, your dog will need even

Select nutritious treats to give to your dog. Remember: they still add calories to his daily diet.

more water. Always have plenty of fresh, cold water available for your Boxer. If possible, do not let your dog drink from anything other than his water bowl. It's better to be safe than sorry!

DON'T FORGET THE TREATS!

You can feed your Boxer treats to reward him for good behavior, during training sessions, or simply to spoil him. It's a pleasure to see a pup enjoying a delicious snack. Treats come in all sorts of sizes and flavors, from fresh-baked biscuits and human treat-inspired cookies to freeze-dried lamb and beef jerky. Some treats also function as edible toothbrushes, scraping off bacteria-ridden plaque from your Boxer's teeth.

You can find treats in pet-supply stores and trendy dog bakeries throughout the country, or you can give your Boxer safe human foods, such as pieces of hot dog, chunks of cheese, or slices of raw beef.

Like regular meals, treats are full of calories. Be sure to calculate them into your pup's overall intake for the day and make sure that treats account for no more than 10 percent of his daily calories. If possible, follow the recommended feeding instructions on the treat package. If you feed your Boxer dog-safe human foods, factor those calories into his daily intake, too.

Supplements: Take 'Em or Leave 'Em?

Supplements add nutrition to your Boxer's diet, and they provide vitamins and minerals. If you feed your dog a well-balanced commercial diet, he probably doesn't need supplements.

Pregnant or lactating females, however, require supplements to provide adequate nutrition to themselves and their litters. Senior Boxers, too, can benefit from formulas for joint function, such as chondroitin and glucosamine.

If you're making your dog's food from scratch, you must supplement his diet with added vitamins and minerals found in herbs, eggs, and Brewer's yeast.

If you feed your Boxer supplements, do so under the watchful eye of your veterinarian or veterinary nutritionist, and never exceed the recommended dosage or substitute supplements for a well-balanced diet. Oversupplementing your Boxer can actually make him sick.

Teething

Some puppies temporarily lose their appetite while they are teething, which usually occurs between four to six months of age. It may help to feed your Boxer softer foods until the teething is complete.

You may want to supplement your dog's diet with a daily tablespoon of cottage cheese or yogurt while he is teething, to ensure that he is getting adequate supplies of calcium. This is safer than adding a supplement, which can lead to a dietary imbalance. The teething process can require a lot of calcium, which is why puppies' ears sometimes temporarily droop during this stage of growth.

As tempting as it may be, don't feed your pooch too many goodies, or your lightweight Boxer will wind up in the heavyweight class!

LIFESTAGE FOODS

Depending on their age, Boxers require varying amounts of calories and nutrients. Pet-food manufacturers know this, so they formulate different diets for different life stages: the puppy stage, the adult stage, and the senior stage.

Puppy Diets

For the first six weeks of life, newborn puppies get all their nourishment from their mothers. When the puppies are about a month old, the breeder introduces small portions of canned meat, slowly weaning the pups from their mother. After they are weaned, typically at eight weeks old, puppies eat foods formulated for growth. These diets help them build strong muscles and bones.

A young puppy up to eight to twelve weeks of age needs to eat up to four meals throughout the day to stimulate growth, keep his metabolism fueled, and prevent hypoglycemia (low blood sugar). As your puppy grows, transition to a twice-a-day routine.

Adult and Senior Diets

Adult dogs eat foods formulated for maintenance, which means they contain the right amount of nutrients to maintain their current size and weight. Once they reach this stage, they only require two meals a day.

As your Boxer ages, his metabolism changes. Older dogs usually exercise less, move more slowly, and sleep more, and this lifestyle change requires a change in diet to compensate. When you feed your slowing senior Boxer an adult diet formulated for maintenance, your dog will gain weight. So, you must adjust his food intake once more. A senior diet contains the right amount of nutrients but fewer calories to prevent obesity. As with other dietary changes, talk to your veterinarian about the right adult and senior formulas for your dog.

IT'S ALL ABOUT PROPORTION

The amount of food you feed your Boxer will depend on the individual dog's growth stage, activity level, and external factors, like temperature or stress. Active dogs or those enduring stress, such as moving or welcoming a new addition to the household, may require more food, depending on the circumstance.

At all times, adjust the amounts you feed based on your dog's appearance. If your Boxer's belly starts bulging, decrease the portion a bit. And if you can see his ribs, add a little more food to his bowl to help him fill out.

A high-calorie diet and a sedentary lifestyle will result in an overweight dog. Adult Boxers that eat too much at mealtime, free-feed, or enjoy too many treats end up consuming too many calories, and weight gain is not far behind. If exercise isn't a part of your dog's daily lifestyle, those extra calories never have a chance to burn off. So keep an eye on your Boxer's weight and consult your veterinarian with any questions.

At a Glance ...

All dogs need a feeding schedule to help them avoid overeating and give them enough fuel to endure the day's activities. Young pups require four daily meals, but Boxers three months and older reduce to two square meals a day.

. . . .

Look for food labeled as "complete and balanced." It means that the formula is approved by the Association of American Feed Control Officials (AAFCO) as nutritious and promotes canine health.

. . . .

Dry, canned, semi-moist, and raw food varieties all have benefits and disadvantages, ranging from taste, shelf life, price point, and caloric intake. Talk to your veterinarian to find out what's best for your Boxer.

. . . .

Lifestage foods have gained popularity in recent years. Following AAFCO guidelines for caloric and nutrient needs, they can help provide the best diet for your puppy, adult, or senior dog.

. . . .

Keep an eye on your Boxer's waistline. An obese dog is an unhealthy dog, and one that's too skinny can end up severely malnourished and ill.

CHAPTER NINE

Grooming Made Simple

Just as you bathe, comb your hair, and brush your teeth daily, your Boxer will require routine maintenance to keep his coat clean and shiny, his nails trimmed, and his breath fresh. Likewise, just as you visit the salon or barber every couple of months, your Boxer may require visits to the groomer for a deep cleanse.

The Boxer has a short, single coat, so his regular upkeep is rather minimal; you can groom him easily at home with just a little instruction, a handful of tools, and a few minutes each day.

Handsome Boxers require standard grooming care, including regular brushing and bathing.

Ear Check

When dogs play outdoors, foreign objects sometimes get stuck in their ears, such as seeds, burrs, and foxtails—anything that tends to stick to fur. Check your Boxer's ears for these things when he comes in from playing outdoors. If left in the ear, they will cause your dog pain and possibly damage his hearing. If you find something in his ear and cannot safely remove it at home, take your dog to the veterinarian ASAP.

GROOMING PREPARATION

Many breeders prepare their pups for grooming when they're still very young. They hold them and coddle them, handling their mouths, paws, eyes, and ears. Most likely, by the time your Boxer meets you, he will be used to being handled. Once you bring your pup home, continue the breeder's work by handling your Boxer every day. Daily grooming rituals, such as the ones listed below, give you the opportunity to handle and inspect your Boxer, so that you can check for abnormalities, such as bumps or cuts. You can also appraise the condition of your dog's paws, ears, eyes, nose, and mouth.

Before you begin actually grooming your Boxer, however, set up a regular grooming space, gather your tools, and accustom your dog to the routine.

Choose a Location

To begin your home-based, Boxer beauty routine, you must first select a location. Dogs like rituals, so choosing one place to regularly groom your Boxer will teach him what to expect and how to behave while you're grooming him.

Because Boxers aren't petite dogs, most people place Boxers on the floor when they clean and brush them, and they use a bathtub or outdoor tub for washing. Whatever location you choose, always place a nonslip pad on the surface—and never leave your Boxer unattended.

Gather Your Tools

Every Boxer household should stock up on basic grooming tools and supplies. You can find them at your local pet-supply store, online, through mail-order catalogs, or through your groomer. Store and organize them in an easily accessible plastic bin or a cosmetic bag for your pup.

• **Shampoo and conditioner:** There are many pet shampoos and conditioners on the market, but choose one formulated for dogs with a short coat. Avoid the shampoo-conditioner combos. They may cut bath time in half, but your

Dog Grooming Shopping List

Here are the items you need to groom your Boxer:

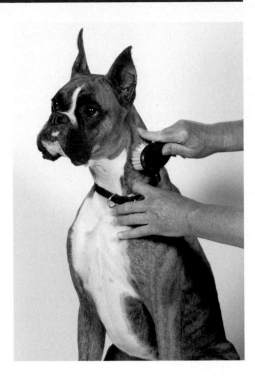

BATHING
- ☐ A handheld spray attachment for your tub or sink
- ☐ A rubber mat for the dog to stand on
- ☐ A tearless dog shampoo and conditioner (don't use human products)
- ☐ Towels (a chamois is best)
- ☐ A pet hair dryer (you can use your own, but set it on cool)
- ☐ Spritz-on dry shampoos (handy in case you need a quick clean-up to get rid of dirt or odor)

BRUSHING COAT
- ☐ Soft pin brush or slicker brush
- ☐ Metal comb

TRIMMING NAILS
- ☐ Dog nail cutters (scissor- or guillotine-type)
- ☐ Nail file (to file down jagged edges)
- ☐ Styptic powder (in case you cut the quick)

BRUSHING TEETH
- ☐ Dog toothbrush or child's toothbrush
- ☐ Dog toothpaste (don't use human toothpaste)

CLEANING EARS
- ☐ Cotton balls or wipes
- ☐ Liquid ear-cleaning solution

WIPING EYES
- ☐ Dog eye wipes or hydrogen peroxide
- ☐ Cotton balls

Did You Know?

The two American Kennel Club-accepted colors for Boxers are fawn (light brown) or brindle (tan with dark brown streaks or stripes). Any white coloring covering more than a third of the entire coat is considered a disqualification by show standards, but Boxers with a lot of white markings still make wonderful pets.

Have the veterinarian check your dog's teeth whenever he goes in for a check up.

Boxer's coat won't be as clean and can develop a sudsy buildup when dry, which will result in dry, flaky skin.

- **Bristle brush:** Resembling a human's hair brush, this brush whisks away debris and polishes your Boxer's coat.
- **Shedding blade:** This tool has bent wire teeth set close together that pull off dead hair.
- **Soft towel or hound glove:** Because the Boxer's coat is short and smooth, a quick wipe-down with a damp towel or glove in between washes will restore the coat's shine and remove any residual dirt.
- **Scissors:** Small scissors are used for trimming the hair around your Boxer's ears, the bottom of the feet, and the anus. Select small-blade scissors that fit your hand comfortably.
- **Nail clippers:** The two basic types of nail clippers are the scissor cut and the guillotine cut. Purchase whichever kind you're most comfortable using.
- **Styptic powder:** Styptic powder, which stops the flow of blood, is good to have on hand for unexpected nail-trimming accidents.
- **Cotton balls:** You'll use these for cleaning out your Boxer's ears and around his eyes—anywhere delicate to the touch.
- **Ear-cleaning solution:** You'll use this cleaning solution on a cotton ball to clean around your pup's ears and inside the folds.
- **Hair dryer:** Although your Boxer's coat is short, you may want to blow dry his coat after bath time to prevent him from chilling. Choose one that has low- and no-heat settings.
- **Toothbrush and dog toothpaste:** Keep your Boxer's teeth plaque- and tartar-free using a soft-bristled toothbrush made for children or dogs, along with dog-specific toothpaste.

Tips for Toes

If your dog spends a lot of time outside on a hard surface, such as cement or pavement, his nails will wear down naturally and will not require trimming as often, except during the winter when he stays inside.

Regardless, you should get your dog accustomed to the nail-trimming procedure at an early age so that he is used to it. Some dogs are especially sensitive about having their feet touched, but if a dog has experienced it since puppyhood, it should not bother him.

A sensitive Boxer may benefit from a nail grinder, which allows you to grind down the nail and prevent accidentally cutting the quick. The device makes quite a racket, so be sure to introduce it to your Boxer when he's young.

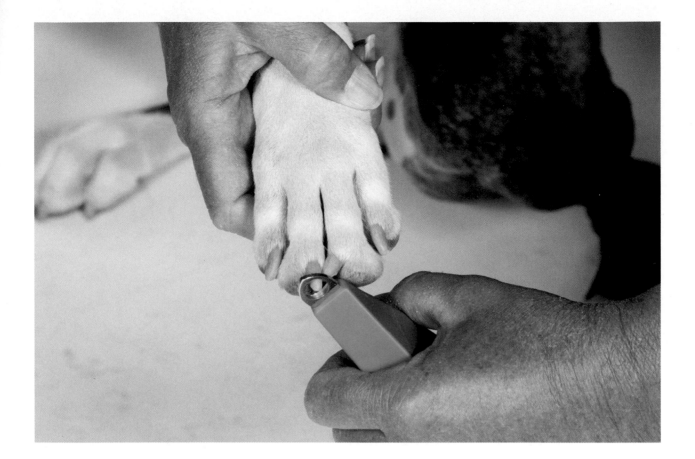

Getting Used to Grooming

You'll have an easier time grooming your Boxer if he's familiar with the designated area and tools you'll be using. Follow these steps to introduce him to this new routine:

1. **Let your Boxer get used to the grooming area.** Allow him to sniff and inspect it for his approval.

2. **Run your hands over his entire body.** Just as you would do when bathing your Boxer, gently give him a massage, feeling every bone, muscle, and tendon. This prepares your dog for grooming and also helps you become more aware of how your dog normally feels. That way, if he develops a lump or injures himself, you'll know right away.

3. **Show your Boxer the grooming tools.** You don't need to use them on your dog just yet; at first, set out the equipment and let him inspect the unfamiliar items. Slowly introduce him to the brush, the toothbrush, and the hair dryer, rewarding him for good behavior.

As you help your Boxer get used to the idea of regular grooming, encourage good behavior by rewarding him with toys and treats. Soon, your Boxer will look forward to those daily brushings and monthly baths!

GETTING DOWN AND DIRTY

You're armed with your grooming tools, and your Boxer knows what to expect. Now the fun begins! Your Boxer will require regular brushing and bathing to keep his skin and coat healthy. Other routine grooming needs include nails trimming, ear cleaning, and teeth brushing. Here's how to perform each task.

If you can hear your Boxer's nails clicking when he walks, it's time to bust out the clippers (a guillotine trimmer is pictured).

Soap It Up

Human soap products like shampoo, bubble bath, and hand soap can damage a dog's coat and skin. Human products are too strong; they remove the protective oils coating the dog's hair and skin that make him water-resistant. On your Boxer, use shampoos made for dogs, a task made easy with all the choices available today!

Dry-bath products, spot cleaners, and wipes can be used between regular baths if necessary. Though they do not replace regular baths, they're handy for touch-ups because they do not require rinsing.

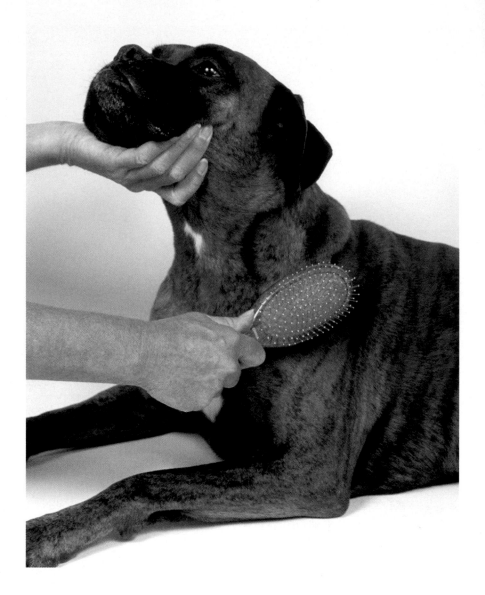

Brushing and Bonding

That short and tight Boxer coat is beautiful. To keep it looking its best, you can expect to brush your dog's fur daily and bathe him monthly.

Oils from sebaceous glands under the skin naturally condition the Boxer's hair and skin. Too much washing can cause dry, flaky skin, but daily brushing releases the oils, keeping the skin and coat healthy. With regular brushing, you'll only need to wash your Boxer once a month or so—unless he meets a skunk or rolls in a puddle of mud!

When brushing your Boxer's coat, follow the same routine each time. That way, he'll know what to expect.

1. Place your Boxer on his designated grooming spot. Begin by using the bristle brush to smooth out his coat and remove any dirt or debris. Always brush in the same direction that the hair grows, brushing from his head toward the tail, then down his sides and legs. Don't forget his belly and face!

2. While you're brushing him, feel along your dog's body for cuts, scrapes, bumps, or irregularities. This is also a great time to check for external parasites, like fleas or ticks.

3. Use the shedding blade to pull off dead hair. Gently rake across your Boxer's body, being careful not to scrape his skin.

Pet Pedicure Procedures

You know your Boxer's nails have grown too long if you hear click-clicking when he walks across the floor. Nail trimming is a grooming ritual that you should do at least once a month. An ideal time to trim your dog's nails is after his bath, when his nails are softened from the warm water. If this isn't possible, plan to trim his nails whenever you have the time.

Like all dogs, your Boxer's nails grow continually and need to be trimmed to keep them at a healthy length. If they grow too long, they can curve inward and cut into the pads of the feet. Long nails can also cause the dog to lose traction because they may prevent the pads from hitting the ground. They can tear upholstery, snag clothing, and cause scratches, too.

Not only does regular trimming keep the nails at a healthy length, but it also gives you the opportunity to inspect your dog's pads for cracks and his toes for splinters or thorns. Your Boxer's pads should be soft yet calloused, depending on his age and activity level. There should be no tender or swollen areas on the paw. If there are, consult your veterinarian for advice.

Before you begin your Boxer's pedicure, look for the quick, which is the vein inside the nail. Using a flashlight or looking at your dog's nails in the sun, you should be able to see the opaque portion in the center base of the nail—that's the

If you're nervous about clipping and filing your dog's nails, your veterinarian or groomer can teach you how to do it safely.

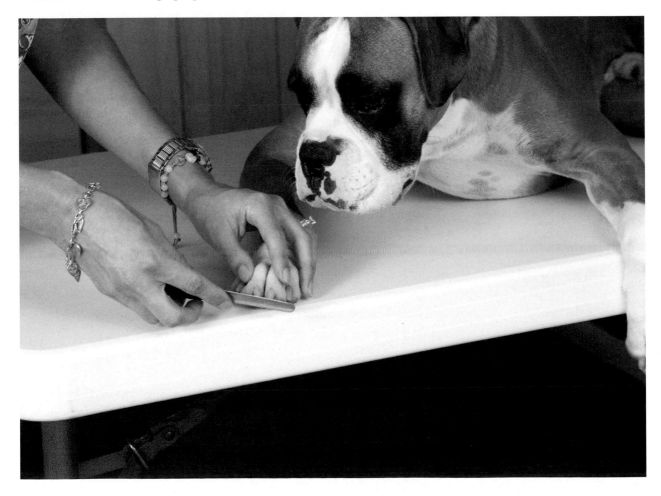

Make your Boxer's annual dental check a breeze. Avoid plaque and tartar buildup on your dog's teeth by regularly brushing them and feeding him crunchy treats and bones.

quick. If your Boxer has dark nails, you may not be able to see the quick. Cut his nails a little at a time, checking for the quick along the nail's edge. Clipping the quick is painful and can cause your Boxer's nail to bleed, so take your time and watch how closely you're cutting. Whenever you trim your dog's nails, keep a container of styptic powder nearby, just in case. If you clip the quick, pour or pack a tiny bit of powder on the nail. It will stop the bleeding.

When you trim your dog's nails for the first few times, enlist the help of another person to steady your Boxer and distract him with a spoonful of peanut butter or a quick ear massage. Having an extra set of hands will be very helpful when your dog starts squirming!

Here's to Clean Ears

The Boxer's cropped ears stand erect, which leaves them prone to dirt, grime, and ear mites. When Boxers play in the yard or meet friends at the dog park, their ears are vulnerable to all sorts of debris. Inspect your dog's ears several times a week and clean them when necessary to keep them healthy.

Ear care will take some getting used to. Your dog might not like to have his ears handled at first. Touch your Boxer's ears often, working with him until he is comfortable with you touching, looking inside, and cleaning his ears.

Taking Care of Teeth

Too often, pet owners fail to consider the condition of their dogs' teeth or provide any dental care at all. Ask your veterinarian to examine your Boxer's teeth at every visit; it might help catch potential problems that could otherwise lead to serious illness. Some dogs' teeth develop tartar because of eating soft food that doesn't require much chewing.

A raw bone can help keep your dog's teeth clean. These bones can be from any large mammal, but readily available beef bones are the most common. Give your dog two large bones a week to provide enough gnawing to scrape off the film that becomes tartar. Don't give your dog cooked bones of any kind because they can splinter apart rather than break off into small chunks and flakes, like raw bones do. Splinters of bone can get stuck in the dog's throat or even puncture his gut lining and cause infections.

Hard, crunchy dog biscuits are another great tool in the arsenal against oral disease. The crunchy texture scrapes the tooth, helping to prevent tartar formation. Best of all, they can be used for rewards any time you're training or want to praise your dog. However, keep in mind that bones and biscuits add calories to your Boxer's diet, so take it easy on the overindulgence.

However, the best way to maintain your dog's dental health is to brush his teeth three or four times a week. Most dogs learn to accept toothbrushing if you slowly accustom them to the brush and reward them often with praise and treats for a job well done. There are several different styles of pet toothbrushes on the market, or you can just use a soft-bristled child's brush. However, don't give your dog human toothpaste—it can make him sick! Instead, look for meat-flavored pet toothpaste. While brushing your Boxer's teeth, be sure to massage his gums, while scrubbing away any food particles on his teeth. Be sure not to press so hard that you make your dog's gums bleed, though. After all, the idea is to help your dog, not hurt him!

GROOMING HEALTH CHECK

Consider your Boxer's grooming sessions as a opportunity to take mental evaluation of his overall health and well being. Note any changes in his appetite or water intake. And search for any out-of-the-ordinary lumps or abrasions while brushing his coat. That way, if you do discover any abnormalities, you can visit the veterinarian for a checkup to avoid the development of any serious ailments. Your constant care and attention to your Boxer's dietary and grooming needs will ensure that you have a happy, healthy, beautiful companion by your side for years to come.

Good Teeth = Good Health

Home dental care is vital to your Boxer's health. Studies prove that good oral hygiene can add three to five years to a dog's life. In other words, brushing your Boxer's teeth means you'll have him around for a lot longer!

At a Glance ...

You've lucked out; Boxers are a relatively care-free breed when it comes to grooming. While those needs are minimal compared to other breeds, your dog will still require regular care and attention to his appearance.

. . . .

Boxers require daily brushing; monthly bathing; and regular nail, ear, and oral care.

. . . .

Start handling your Boxer while he's still a puppy and introduce him to all of the grooming tools to accustom him to the sights, sounds, and feel of the grooming routine before you begin.

. . . .

While brushing and bathing your dog, look and feel all over his body for bumps, cuts, and any other abnormalities. If you find something troubling, consult your veterinarian.

CHAPTER TEN

A Lifetime of **Good Health**

The veterinarian plays an important role in your family's life. Your vet not only will help keep your Boxer healthy but also will help you become a better dog owner. To find a good health-care provider for your Boxer, consult your breeder, other pet owners, and local Boxer breed clubs. Then, it's up to you to select the veterinarian who you feel most comfortable with and who can provide the best care for your Boxer. It's your responsibility to stay on top of

your Boxer's care schedule and take him in for yearly vet checkups. Together with a knowledgeable veterinarian, you can tackle any health issue that may arise.

Take your puppy to the veterinarian within three or four days of bringing him home. Show the vet any health records of vaccinations and wormings from your breeder. The vet will conduct a thorough physical exam to make sure your Boxer is in good health and will work out a schedule for vaccinations, micro-chipping, and regular puppy visits. A good veterinarian will be gentle and affectionate with a new pup and will do everything possible to make sure your Boxer is neither frightened nor intimidated.

VACCINATE!

Puppies need a series of vaccinations to protect them from many potentially lethal canine diseases. Vaccine protocol varies among veterinarians, but most recommend a series of three combination shots given at three- to four-week intervals. Your puppy should have had his first shot before he left his breeder.

Canine vaccines are classified as "core" and "non-core." Every dog should receive core vaccines, but non-core ones are optional. The value of non-core vaccines is dependent on your dog's environment and lifestyle. Ask your vet and your dog's breeder when deciding which vaccinations are necessary. There is a wealth of information available on the subject of canine vaccination for anyone willing to do the research. The websites for the American Animal Hospital Association and the American Veterinary Medical Association are great places to start. The AAHA offers a report on vaccinations, which is available to download at www.aahanet.org/Library/CanineVaccine.aspx. The AVMA answers frequently asked questions about pet vaccinations at www.avma.org/issues/vaccination.

CORE Vaccines
Check with your vet, but all puppies should receive vaccines for the following diseases.

CONDITION	TREATMENT	PROGNOSIS	VACCINE NEEDED
ADENOVIRUS-2 (immunizes against Adenovirus-1, the agent of infectious canine hepatitis)	No curative therapy for infectious hepatitis; treatment geared toward minimizing neurologic effects, shock, hemorrhage, secondary infections	Self-limiting but cross-protects against infectious hepatitis, which is highly contagious and can be mild to rapidly fatal	Recommended
DISTEMPER	No specific treatment; supportive treatment (IV fluids, antibiotics)	High mortality rates	Highly recommended
PARVOVIRUS-2	No specific treatment; supportive treatment (IV fluids, antibiotics)	Highly contagious to young puppies; high mortality rates	Highly recommended
RABIES	No treatment	Fatal	Required

The newest guidelines from the AAHA recommend that puppies complete a DHPP (distemper, hepatitis [adenovirus], parainfluenza, parvovirus) vaccination series. Combination shots vary, and a single injection may contain anywhere from five to eight vaccines in one shot, all of which your puppy may not need.

Many veterinarians believe that the potency in high-combination vaccines can negatively compromise a puppy's immature immune system. They recommend fewer vaccines in one shot or even separating vaccines into individual injections. The wisest and most conservative course of action is to administer only one shot in a single visit, rather than giving two or three shots at the same time. Discuss your Boxer's particular needs with your vet before vaccinations are administered.

It is your responsibility to find a veterinarian who can provide the best care possible for your Boxer. Check with your breeder or local Boxer club for a list of trusted vets.

Core Vaccines

Distemper: This highly contagious disease is transmitted by direct contact with fluids from infected dogs. After exposure, the onset of symptoms can vary from one to three weeks. Symptoms may include depression, loss of appetite, vomiting, diarrhea, discharge from the nose and eyes, seizures, and paralysis. Bronchitis and pneumonia are common secondary complications.

Parvovirus: Also highly contagious, this viral infection is transmitted by contact with traces of infected fecal matter. It is easily spread to dogs by humans carrying the virus on their hands, shoes, or clothing. Symptoms become evident two to seven days after exposure. Dogs of all ages are susceptible, but puppies are at greatest risk. The virus attacks the gastrointestinal system, causing sudden and severe vomiting, bloody diarrhea, dehydration, and shock. It can be fatal in small puppies, despite treatment.

Adenovirus: Infectious canine hepatitis is a highly contagious viral disease spread by direct or indirect contact with urine and feces of infected dogs. Symptoms include conjunctivitis, tonsillitis, loss of appetite, jaundice, and abdominal tenderness due to gall bladder and liver inflammation.

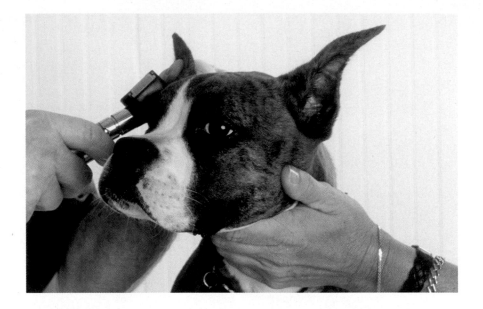

Finding a Good Vet

When selecting a vet for your Boxer, answer these questions:

■ Does the clinic belong to a certification program such as the American Animal Hospital Association (www.aahanet.org)?

■ Is emergency care offered?

■ Are hospitalized pets monitored overnight?

■ Does the vet office offer any specialties such as orthopedics or acupuncture?

■ What are the regular office hours, as well as emergency clinic hours?

■ What payment options are accepted? If you have health insurance for your Boxer, make sure your vet's office accepts your insurance plan.

Rabies: This well-known viral infection is carried and spread through the saliva of infected individuals. The virus attacks the central nervous system. Symptoms include disorientation, headache, fretfulness, drooling, seizures, and hallucinations.

Non-Core Vaccines

Bordetella: Also known as kennel cough, Bordetella is a highly contagious airborne disease caused by bacterium, virus, or a combination of infectious agents. It is the canine equivalent of human whooping cough. The incubation period can range from twelve to fourteen days. It can develop into a serious secondary infection or pneumonia in puppies. Dogs at high risk should be re-vaccinated twice yearly.

Lyme disease: Spread by deer ticks, Lyme disease can present itself in symptoms that vary from mild to severe, possibly including limping, joint pain, fever, loss of appetite, and swollen lymph nodes. If you live in a high-risk area, your vet may recommend vaccinating against Lyme disease.

PESKY PESTS

Inevitably, at some point your Boxer will get fleas. Other less-common parasites are problematic, as well. Dealing with these parasites is simply a common side effect of taking your dog outside to play and go to the bathroom. Luckily, canine pest-control is easy to treat.

Fleas: As long as there have been dog owners to notice it, fleas have been a problem for dogs and other pets. Not only do they cause your dog to bite and scratch himself silly, but they can also cause disease. Your Boxer will undoubtedly get fleas at some point in his life, if not on more than one occasion. It's difficult to avoid because Boxers love to spend so much time outside—and fleas love to spend so much time on dogs! Luckily there are many ways to fight flea infestation. It may be difficult to prevent, but it is relatively simple to cure.

Because fleas travel on and off their hosts, you'll need to treat both your dog and your home to get rid of them. The most effective method of flea control is a two-stage approach: first kill the adult fleas, then control the development of pre-adult fleas. Treat your home with an insect growth regulator spray and an insecticide to kill adult fleas, making sure you cover all carpets, furniture, bedding, hidden crevices, and anywhere else your dog likes to spend time.

Once you've taken care of your home, it's time to treat your dog. Liquid treatments are popular—you squeeze the medication onto your Boxer's back between the shoulders. The liquid drops spread throughout the hair and skin to kill the adult fleas. Some flea treatments are in pill form, which you give to your dog in his food each month. It's best to ask your veterinarian which medicines are right for fighting your dog's fleas. Discuss safe flea treatment options with your veterinarian before administering any by yourself.

Ticks: Ticks are a concern for active dogs that like to spend time outdoors. Ticks can cause diseases, such as Lyme disease (borreliosis) and Rocky Mountain spotted fever, which sometimes spread to humans as well. Talk to your vet to find out if ticks are a major concern for your region. He or she will have information

Other Vaccines and Treatment

Depending on where you live and your dog's needs, the following ailments and diseases can be treated through your veterinarian.

CONDITION	TREATMENT	PROGNOSIS	RECOMMENDATION
BORDETELLA (KENNEL COUGH)	Keep warm; humidify room; moderate exercise	Highly contagious; rarely fatal in healthy dogs; easily treated	Optional; prevalence varies; vaccine may be linked to acute reactions; low efficacy
FLEA AND TICK	Topical and ingestible	Highly contagious	Highly recommended
HEARTWORM	Arsenical compound; rest; restricted exercise	Widely occurring infections; preventive programs available regionally; successful treatment after early detection	Preventive treatment highly recommended
INTESTINAL WORMS	Dewormer; home medication regimen	Good with prompt treatment	Highly recommended
LYME DISEASE	Antibiotics	Can't completely eliminate the organism, but can be controlled in most cases	Recommended only for dogs with high risk of exposure to deer ticks
PARAINFLUENZA	Rest; humidify room; moderate exercise	Highly contagious; mild; self-limiting; rarely fatal	Optional but recommended; doesn't block infection, but lessens clinical signs
PERIODONTITIS	Dental cleaning; extractions; repair	Excellent, but involves anesthesia	Recommended

Your veterinarian will recommend a series of combination vaccines, which will protect your Boxer from serious diseases, such as distemper and rabies. Ask your vet about non-core vaccines suggested for your region.

for how to protect your Boxer, as well as be able to discuss whether the Lyme disease vaccine is in your dog's best interest.

Mites: Regularly check your Boxer for ear mites. They can't be seen, but a brown discharge with some odor from the ear is a clear indication that they're there. If you see these telltale signs, go to your veterinarian for a suitable ear treatment.

Worms: Dogs can also carry internal parasites in the form of worms. Roundworms (ascarids) are the most common, and they may cause mild diarrhea or vomiting. The worms look like strands of spaghetti in the feces or vomit. Tapeworms are detected in the dog's feces; they resemble moving grains of rice. Both roundworms and tapeworms are easily treated.

Support Canine Health Research

The American Kennel Club Canine Health Foundation (www.akcchf.org) raises money to support canine health research. The foundation makes grants to fund:

- Identifying the cause(s) of disease
- Earlier, more accurate diagnosis
- Developing screening tests for breeders
- Accurate, positive prognosis
- Effective, efficient treatment

The AKC Canine Health Foundation (AKC CHF) also supports educational programs that bring scientists together to discuss their work and develop new collaborations to further advance canine health.

The AKC created the AKC Canine Health Foundation in 1995 to raise funds to support canine health research. Each year, the AKC CHF allocates $1.5 million to new canine health research projects.

How You Can Help: If you have an AKC-registered dog, submit his DNA sample (cheek swab or blood sample) to the Canine Health Information Center (CHIC) DNA databank (www.caninehealthinfo.org). Encourage regular health testing by breeders, get involved with your local dog club, and support the efforts to host health education programs. And, if possible, make a donation.

For information, contact the AKC Canine Health Foundation, P.O. Box 900061, Raleigh, NC 27675-9061 or check out the website at www.akcchf.org.

Hookworms and heartworms are more serious. Hookworms cause tar-like or bloody stool. Heartworms are transmitted by mosquitoes; symptoms include loss of appetite, weight loss, and lethargy. Discuss preventive treatment with your vet. Some monthly treatments work to protect against heartworms and hookworms, as well as some of the other common internal parasites.

Depending on where you live, your vet will advise you on the best way to protect your dog from various pests. Owners of outdoorsy breeds like the Boxer must take extra precautions to avoid ticks and mosquitoes whenever possible. For dogs of all breeds and sizes, however, routine worming is essential throughout their life. Be sure to discuss all parasite-management options with your vet before starting any treatment.

COMMON BOXER AILMENTS

Responsible breeders work diligently to try to reduce or elimnate all health risks; however, Boxers do seem to have a predisposition to some ailments. Such conditions include heart disease (aortic stenosis and cardiomyopathy), neurological Degenerative Myelopathy (DM), hip dysplasia, thyroid deficiency (resulting in thyroid malfunction or tumors), and various other cancers (including brain, heart, spleen, mammary, testes, blood, lymph system, skin lesions, and other organs).

Often diagnosis of these conditions will result in successful treatment or symptomatic relief, which is why frequent veterinary care is so vital to the Boxer's ongoing health. Refer to the American Boxer Club (www.americanboxerclub.org) for the most up-to-date, breed-specific health information, as well as for details on DNA swabs and blood tests available to test for certain health-related concerns.

WEIGHT WATCHERS

Preventive health care also includes choosing a healthy diet for your Boxer and properly maintaining his weight. Make small modifications to his diet to keep him at his ideal weight, rather than waiting until the situation calls for drastic measures. Discuss with your veterinarian before making a big change to your Boxer's diet.

Feel your dog's torso to deterine his healthy weight. You should be able to feel his ribs beneath a thin layer of muscle with very gentle pressure on his rib cage. When viewing your dog from above, you should see a definite waistline; from the side, he should have an obvious tuck-up in his abdomen.

Keep a record of your Boxer's weight from each annual vet visit. Adjust his food portions if he gains too much weight. Switch to a "light," "senior," or lower-

Tranquilizer Caution

All Boxer owners should know that Boxers have a serious reaction to a tranquilizing drug called Acepromazine. "Ace" is a pre-anesthetic frequently used before surgery. It has been shown to cause a serious heart arrhythmia when administered to some Boxers. This drug is also commonly prescribed as an oral tranquilizer for dogs traveling by car or air. If your Boxer ever needs a surgical procedure or tranquilizer, be sure to discuss with your veterinarian which drugs will be used.

A PIECE OF HISTORY

In 1995, the American Boxer Charitable Foundation was founded by a small group of individuals with the distinct goal of raising money to fund research into health-related issues facing the Boxer breed. The foundation has raised more than $500,000 in research funds to date.

Spay/Neuter

Should you or shouldn't you? This is a question that concerns every Boxer owner. If you are keeping a Boxer solely as a companion and guard, neutering and spaying remain an excellent choice, as it will relieve you of many of the complications associated with unaltered dogs.

Male dogs that remain intact tend to wander away from home in search of females in heat, and they often lift their legs on bushes and shrubs to mark their territory.

Likewise, females go through twice-annual estrus (heat) periods, which can be messy and problematic to owners. Certainly unwanted pregnancies are another disadvantage of keeping unaltered dogs.

The ultimate decision rests with you—discuss the matter with your breeder and veterinarian.

calorie dog food formula and increase his exercise. Proper exercise goes hand-in-hand with diet management for optimal health care. Daily exercise will ensure that a puppy has an acceptable outlet for his energy, and it will keep a senior dog active and alert.

Excessive weight is especially hard on older dogs with creaky joints. A senior Boxer that is sedentary will become out of shape quickly. Walking and running (slower for older dogs) are still the best workouts for health maintenance. Tailor your dog's exercise to fit his age and physical condition.

Sending your Boxer out to amuse himself in a fenced yard is not an acceptable solution. Most dogs find this boring and will sooner or later resort to bad habits like digging or barking to keep themselves amused. Instead, schedule some daily interactive exercise such as a couple of brisk daily walks or runs and regular play sessions with you. Flip to chapter 11 for more ideas of sports and other physical activities to get involved in with your dog.

Annual Health Exam

Most veterinarians recommend at least yearly routine checkups as your Boxer grows up. Your vet will administer any necessary booster vaccinations and give your dog a thorough physical exam, including checking your dog's eyes, ears, and heart. A dental evaluation and teeth cleaning may also be part of the services.

An annual exam not only helps to spot many problems before symptoms are obvious, but it will also reassure you about your dog's health. The precise nature of the exam may vary, depending on your dog's age and condition. For instance, your vet may recommend blood tests, urinalysis, and X-rays for senior dogs or as a follow up to any unusual findings, but only order a blood test for a young Boxer. Fecal testing to detect internal parasites should be done yearly. Parasites don't always cause obvious symptoms, but they will become worse if left untreated. Discuss with your vet whether your Boxer needs booster shots or full anesthesia dental cleaning. These treatments are not without risk, so make sure they are necessary before agreeing to them.

Make sure to point out any small bumps and growths you find on your dog; they can be biopsied and tested to identify any possible early stages of cancer. Early detection and biopsy analysis are vital in determining the best course of treatment.

After your Boxer reaches the age of seven, your vet may recommend scheduling twice-yearly health exams. Many age-related health disorders, such as heart or kidney disease, respond well to early treatment. And a vet exam may alert you to them before any obvious symptoms arise.

A TRIP TO THE DENTIST

The American Veterinary Dental Society (www.avds-online.org) states that by age three, 80 percent of dogs exhibit signs of gum disease. (Quick, look at your dog's teeth!) Symptoms include yellow and brown build-up of tartar along the gumline; red, inflamed gums; and persistent bad breath. If neglected, these conditions will allow bacteria to accumulate in your dog's mouth and enter your dog's bloodstream through those damaged gums, increasing the risk for disease in vital organs such as the heart, liver, and kidneys. It's also known that periodontal disease is a major contributor to kidney disease, which is a common cause of death in older dogs—all this is highly preventable.

Ask your veterinarian to examine your Boxer's teeth and gums during his annual checkup to make sure they are clean and healthy. The vet may recommend professional cleaning if there is excessive plaque build-up.

During the other 364 days of the year, you are your dog's dentist. You can do your part in your Boxer's home oral care by regularly brushing his teeth and providing plenty of dry kibble or crunchy treats, as well as abrasive chew toys. Find further information about canine oral care in chapter 9. Start the brushing process with gentle gum massages when your pup is very young so he will learn to tolerate and even enjoy the process.

YOUR RESPONSIBILITY

Your Boxer's health is in your hands between those annual visits to the vet. Be aware of any changes in his appearance or behavior. Things to consider:

A yearly, routine checkup is vital to the health and well-being of your Boxer. Even if your Boxer seems healthy, it is important to have a veterinarian ensure that your dog's health is on track.

Has your Boxer gained a few too many pounds or suddenly lost weight? Are his teeth clean and white, or does he need some plaque treatment? Is he urinating more frequently or drinking more water than usual? Does he strain during bowel movements? Are there any changes in his appetite? Does he appear short of breath, lethargic, or overly tired? Have you noticed limping or any sign of joint stiffness?

These are all signs of serious health problems, which you should discuss with your veterinarian as soon as they appear. This is especially important for a senior dog because even a subtle change can be a sign of something serious. When in doubt, call your vet.

At a Glance ...

A good canine health plan starts with your veterinarian and continues at home. Preventive care is the best way to take care of your Boxer.

. . . .

Take your dog for regular, annual checkups to ensure his health is on track. And keep an eye out for any abnormalities in between visits.

. . . .

For the most up-to-date Boxer health information, refer to the breed's parent club, the American Boxer Club, at www.americanboxerclub.org.

. . . .

Oral care is an important part of overall canine health—and it is unfortunately too often overlooked. Brush your dog's teeth regularly, and give him crunchy food and treats as an added aid. Have your vet examine your Boxer's teeth during his annual checkups to catch any problems early.

. . . .

Watch for any unusual behavior or other signs of illness from your Boxer, and contact your vet if you're ever unsure.

CHAPTER ELEVEN

Keeping Your Boxer Active

A world of fun and exciting sports and other activities await your well-trained and active Boxer. Best of all, there is plenty you can do together to develop your bond, while also exercising to stay healthy. Through his intensity, interest level, and extra willingness to work, your Boxer will let you know what activities he enjoys the most. And given the proper guidance and practice, your dog will shine in these sports.

GET INVOLVED

If competitive canine sports intrigue you, join your local Boxer club or the national breed parent club, the American Boxer Club (www.americanboxerclub .org). These clubs often host specialty shows just for Boxers, which usually include conformation, obedience, and agility trials. Even if you don't intend to enter your Boxer in any of the events, a specialty show is like a festival for Boxer lovers, complete with booths, experts, and entertainment all day long.

If your Boxer is six months of age or older and is registered with the American Kennel Club, he is eligible to compete in a conformation show. The purpose of the show is to select which representatives in a breed are ideal for breeding. As such, only unaltered dogs can compete in conformation shows. Altered dogs can participate in other AKC events, such as obedience trials and the Canine Good Citizen® program.

Clubs usually send out newsletters, and some organize training days and seminars for those who want to learn more about Boxers. To locate the breed club nearest you, contact the American Kennel Club, which furnishes the rules and regulations for all these events plus general dog registration and other basic requirements of dog ownership.

To find out about dogs shows in your area and learn about all the events the AKC has to offer, go to www.akc.org/events.

If your Boxer follows cues to the letter, agility may be just the sport for him. Agility requires high energy, intelligence, and patience from both dog and owner.

Dog Shows

In conformation shows, or "dog shows" as they are commonly called, judges evaluate dogs and select the one that best "conforms" to the breed standard. During a show, the dogs first compete against members of their own breed, earning a Best of Breed title. The winner of that contest competes with other Best of Breed winners in his group—Boxers compete in the Working group. Finally, the dogs chosen first in each group compete for Best in Show. The winners take home points toward their titles and colorful ribbons to decorate their owners' walls.

The American Kennel Club offers three types of conformation shows:

• **All-breed shows:** These shows are most often televised and offer competitions for more than 170 breeds and varieties recognized by the AKC.

• **Specialty shows:** Often hosted by breed clubs, these shows highlight one specific breed or varieties of a breed.

• **Group shows:** These shows are limited to dogs within a particular group, such as the Non-Sporting, Hound, or Herding groups. Boxers fall within the Working group.

The AKC offers further information about how to get involved in conformation shows at www.akc.org/events/conformation.

Obedience

If your Boxer excelled in his puppy kindergarten class, basic obedience-training course, and Canine Good Citizen® test, he may be an ideal candidate for obedience competitions. Obedience trials require your Boxer to perform specific exercises that show how well your dog obeys your cues. According to the AKC, obedience is the foundation for all dog sports. To enter an obedience trial, you must submit an official AKC entry form to the trial secretary. After the entry period closes, you'll receive a judging schedule for each class.

Learn more about the AKC's obedience program, the sport's history, and the various titles your dog can earn at www.akc.org/events/obedience.

Tracking

Tracking, a type of obedience trial, tests a dog's ability to recognize and trace a human's scent, much like dogs do during search-and-rescue operations. Just because your Boxer has a short snout doesn't mean he can't track a scent!

The sport, originally called Obedience Test Field Trials, began in 1936, and since then, it has been refined to include more specific tracking exercises, as well as adjusted to account for ever-diminishing fields and open spaces.

Tracking is great exercise for your Boxer and a creative opportunity for the two of you to work together in a fun environment. Your kennel club can provide more information about training for and participating in these challenging competitions. Go to www.akc.org/events/tracking for more information about the AKC's tracking events.

Agility Trials

This fast-growing canine sport challenges your dog's nimble feet as he runs through a series of timed obstacle courses. Responding to your cues as you run

Get involved in local AKC events such as rally and conformation and build a strong bond between you and your Boxer. It's also a great way to meet other Boxer owners and their dogs.

Did You Know?

The breed's national parent club, the American Boxer Club, holds national and regional specialty shows every year.

Interested in conformation? Attend a specialty show hosted by your local Boxer club. You'll get to meet Boxer handlers, breeders, and other owners who can help you learn more about the sport.

alongside him, your Boxer races through jumps, tunnels, weave poles, and other obstacles. In agility competition, the winning dog completes the obstacle course in the fastest time and loses the fewest points due to technical mistakes.

The sport began in England in 1978. It made its official appearance in the United States, when the AKC held its first agility trial in 1994. Part of the lure of this fun sport is that dogs of all sizes can compete. The judges adjust the obstacles' heights and vary the time allowance, depending on the breed. People of all ages can compete, too, making it a sport for just about any fancier.

Practicing for this event can be a challenge because the obstacles take up considerable space, but clubs across the country conduct practice matches. So, if this sport interests you, talk to your local kennel club for more information. If your Boxer is full of energy, training him in agility can be a great outlet for that energy. This type of training is also an excellent opportunity to strengthen your bond with your dog, as you must learn to work closely together as a team. Learn more about the AKC's agility events at www.akc.org/events/agility.

Rally

Combining the precision of obedience with the fast-paced style of agility, rally is the AKC's newest canine sport offering. Developed after the rally style of car racing, this sport requires the dog/handler team to navigate through a course made up of directional signs. Each course is unique, to keep competitors on their toes. It's great for everyone from first-time competitors to seasoned veterans.

If you choose to be your Boxer's handler in rally, you and your dog will get to show off your skills together. Similar to obedience trials, this sport showcases how well your dog obeys what you ask of him. However, rally's performance rules are a bit more relaxed than those of obedience trials. On the rally course, you can expect to work your way together through ten to twenty stations, each requiring your team to show off a different skill. For more information about rally competitions, visit www.akc.org/events/rally.

Junior Scholarships

The American Kennel Club shows its commitment to supporting young people in their interest in purebred dogs by awarding thousands of dollars of scholarships to those competing in Junior Showmanship. The scholarships range from $1,000 to $5,000 and are based on a person's academic achievements and his or her history with purebred dogs. Learn more at www.akc.org/kids_juniors.

AMERICAN KENNEL CLUB™

The AKC Code of Sportsmanship

- Sportsmen respect the history, traditions, and integrity of the sport of purebred dogs.
- Sportsmen commit themselves to values of fair play, honesty, courtesy, and vigorous competition, as well as winning and losing with grace.
- Sportsmen refuse to compromise their commitment and obligation to the sport of purebred dogs by injecting personal advantage or consideration into their decisions or behavior.
- The sportsman judge judges only on the merits of the dogs and considers no other factors.
- The sportsman judge or exhibitor accepts constructive criticism.
- The sportsman exhibitor declines to enter or exhibit under a judge where it might reasonably appear that the judge's placements could be based on something other than the merits of the dogs.
- The sportsman exhibitor refuses to compromise the impartiality of a judge.
- The sportsman respects the American Kennel Club's bylaws, rules, regulations, and policies governing the sport of purebred dogs.
- Sportsmen find that vigorous competition and civility are not inconsistent and are able to appreciate the merit of their competition and the efforts of competitors.
- Sportsmen welcome, encourage, and support newcomers to the sport.
- Sportsmen will deal fairly with all those who trade with them.
- Sportsmen are willing to share honest and open appraisals of both the strengths and weaknesses of their breeding stock.
- Sportsmen spurn any opportunity to take personal advantage of positions offered or bestowed upon them.
- Sportsmen always consider as paramount the welfare of their dogs.
- Sportsmen refuse to embarrass the sport, the American Kennel Club, or themselves while taking part in the sport.

Competing in AKC trials and events takes time and dedication. To get a head start, be sure to enroll your Boxer in training classes, such as puppy kindergarten and obedience classes at a young age.

A LITTLE ORGANIZED FUN

Besides participating in obedience trials, Boxers also love to have some fun! You can engage your dog in both organized and spontaneous sporting events. Consider playing a fun game of Frisbee or fetch in the local dog park, hiking some scenic trails, or trolling the beach for shells with your best canine companion. It doesn't get much better!

Two other organized sports that you and your Boxer may find fun and challenging are flyball and freestyle.

Fun on the Fly

Flyball is a timed relay race that pits two teams of four dogs against each other. In this game, at the signal, the first dog must run over a series of hurdles to a box of tennis balls and jump on a lever to send a ball flying. The dog then catches the ball and runs with it to his owner, which signals the next dog in line to start the course. This fun activity can burn a lot of Boxer energy!

The sport currently enjoys international recognition, with clubs throughout the world. If your Boxer loves to catch tennis balls, seek out a flyball club in your area. You can find a list of clubs on the websites for the National American Flyball Association (www.flyball.org) and the United Flyball League International (www.u-fli.com).

Dancing with Dogs

Canine freestyle is a human-dog choreographed dance that incorporates obedience commands such as *sit* and *stay*. The object of the sport is for you and your dog to display innovative and original dance using movements to showcase teamwork, creativity, costumes, and style—all while interpreting the theme of the music.

Today, several organizations regulate competitive canine freestyle, including the Canine Freestyle Federation (www.canine-freestyle.org), World Canine Freestyle Organization (www.worldcaninefreestyle.org), and Musical Dog Sport Association (www.musicaldogsport.org). Competitions differ from group to group, but generally, titles are awarded to high scores in technical merit and artistic impression.

SERVING WITH A SMILE

Thanks to his character, strength, and spot-on senses, the Boxer happily performs in a range of service-dog and assistance-dog capacities. The Boxer has historically served in the military, joined the ranks of K9 police services, and assisted the legal forces of many nations. In homes, the Boxer's steady temperament and affinity for human touch have made the breed a superior choice for therapy work. Boxers also serve their community in various service dog, guide dog, and hearing dog roles.

Assistance dogs help their handlers with their specific needs: guide dogs help the blind, hearing dogs assist the deaf, and service dogs lend a hand to those who are physically disabled. Donning their orange vests, U-shaped harnesses, or backpacks, respectively, these four-legged helpers give their handlers freedom to function normally in society.

Consider volunteering to raise or foster Boxer puppies for various programs, such as The Assistance Dog Institute (www.assistancedog.org) or Assistance Dogs of America Inc. (www.adai.org).

Boxers in Therapy

For Boxers (and their owners) that enjoy giving back to their community, becoming a therapy dog is an opportunity to bring joy to anyone from children to seniors who have limited mobility beyond their hospitals or nursing homes.

A well-behaved Boxer that has passed his Canine Good Citizen® test is well on his way to becoming a therapy dog, if you so choose. Different from assistance dogs that help their blind or otherwise disabled owners, some therapy dogs make informal visits to people in nursing homes and hospitals, while others participate

Therapy Dog Must-Haves

Organizations such as Therapy Dogs International and the Delta Society evaluate potential therapy dogs and train those that show promise. Therapy dogs must:

• Display sound temperament.

• Be patient, confident, and at ease in a variety of circumstances, from busy hospital wards to sedate retirement homes.

• Thrive on human contact because one of their main purposes is to allow people to pet and dote on them.

If you think your Boxer fits the bill, then consider getting involved in therapy work and helping to make a big difference in other people's lives.

in more structured sessions with people who are receiving physical therapy or coordination lessons.

If you think your Boxer would make a great therapy dog, the American Kennel Club can help get you started. There are many programs devoted to canine therapy work. Contact the following organizations for more information to get started.

• **AKC's Canine Good Citizen® program:** Rewarding dogs that have good manners at home and in the community, this two-part program requires dogs to pass a ten-step test to receive a certificate touting the dog's preparedness for positive interaction in your community. It's the first step toward reaching out to others in your community together with your dog. Learn more about the program at www.akc.org/events/cgc.

• **AKC Therapy Dog program:** New to the AKC's list of offerings, this program recognizes all AKC dog-and-owner teams that have volunteered their time and helped people in therapy work. It awards an official AKC Therapy Dog title (AKC ThD) to dogs that have been certified by recognized therapy dog associations and have worked to improve the lives of the people they've visited. Get more information at www.akc.org/akctherapydog.

• **Delta Society:** Matching people with mental and physical disabilities and patients in health-care facilities together with professionally trained animals, this international nonprofit organization helps to improve patients' health and well-being. Learn more about the Delta Society at www.deltasociety.com.

• **Therapy Dogs Inc.:** For members involved in animal-assisted volunteer activities, this organization provides registration, support, and insurance. Visit www.therapydogs.com for more information.

• **Therapy Dogs International:** Helping qualified handlers and their therapy dogs visit facilities and institutions where therapy dogs are needed, this

Junior Showmanship

Junior Showmanship classes, which are open to children ages 9 to 18 years old, offer the opportunity for budding fanciers to develop their handling skills, learn about good sportsmanship, and learn about dogs and dog shows.

The competitions include handling and performance events, similar to those offered for adults. Judges evaluate the children's handling methods, rather than the animals, although the dogs do need to be registered with the AKC.

If your child shows interest in Junior Showmanship, encourage it! Many junior handlers continue their love of dogs to become professional handlers, veterinarians, breeders, and trainers as they grow older. Learn more about Junior Showmanship at www.akc.org/kids_juniors.

nonprofit volunteer group is always looking for a few good dogs. Get more information at www.tdi-dog.org.

THE BOTTOM LINE

Above all else, just get out and have fun with your Boxer—whether that means participating in an organized sporting event, visiting people in need, or simply throwing around a Frisbee in the park.

Your dog will love spending time with you, and you benefit from staying active, too! Together, you and your Boxer will be a healthy and happy team for years to come.

Your Boxer will be happiest by your side, so remember to set aside enough time to regularly play, exercise, and enjoy each others' company.

At a Glance ...

Your highly trainable, active Boxer will need plenty of exercise and can excel in many sports and other activities. Check out the American Kennel Club's website (www.akc.org) and consider joining the national American Boxer Club (www.americanboxerclub.com) or a local regional breed club to find out how to get involved in organized canine sports.

· ·

Conformation, agility, tracking, obedience, and rally are just a few of the events that the AKC offers for Boxers and their owners.

· ·

Therapy work is an excellent opportunity to have your Canine Good Citizen®-tested dog make a real difference in the lives of those around him.

· ·

Regardless of what activities you choose to do with your Boxer, it's most important that you both have fun and stay healthy together.

Resources

BOOKS

The American Kennel Club's Meet the Breeds: Dog Breeds from A to Z (Irvine, California: BowTie Press, 2011) The ideal puppy buyer's guide, the 2012 edition of this book has all you need to know about each breed currently recognized by the AKC.

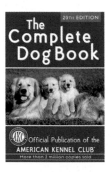

The Complete Dog Book, 20th edition (New York: Ballantine Books, 2006) This official publication of the AKC, first published in 1929, includes the complete histories and breed standards of 153 recognized breeds, as well as information on general care and the dog sport.

The Complete Dog Book for Kids (New York: Howell Book House, 1996) Specifically geared toward young people, this official publication of the AKC presents 149 breeds and varieties, as well as introductory owners' information.

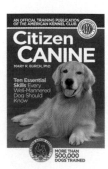

Citizen Canine: Ten Essential Skills Every Well-Mannered Dog Should Know by Mary R. Burch, PhD (Freehold, New Jersey: Kennel Club Books, 2010) This official AKC publication is the definitive guide to the AKC's Canine Good Citizen program, recognized as the gold standard of behavior for dogs, with more than half a million dogs trained.

DOGS: The First 125 Years of the American Kennel Club (Freehold, New Jersey: Kennel Club Books, 2009) This official AKC publication presents an authoritative complete history of the AKC, including detailed information not found in any other volume.

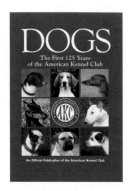

Dog Heroes of September 11: A Tribute to America's Search and Rescue Dogs, 2nd edition, by Nona Kilgore Bauer (Irvine, California: BowTie Press, 2011) The only publication to salute the canines that served the nation in the recovery missions following the terrorists' attacks on America, this book serves as a lasting tribute to these noble American heroes.

The Original Dog Bible: The Definitive Source for All Things Dog, 2nd edition, by Kristin Mehus-Roe (Irvine, California: BowTie Press, 2009) This 831-page magnum opus includes more than 250 breed profiles, hundreds of color photographs, and a wealth of information on every dog topic imaginable—thousands of practical tips on grooming, training, care, and much more.

PERIODICALS

American Kennel Club Gazette

Every month since 1889, serious dog fanciers have looked to the *Gazette* for authoritative advice on training, showing, breeding, and canine health. Each issue includes the breed columns section, written by experts from the respective breed clubs. Now only available electronically.

AKC Family Dog

This is a bi-monthly magazine for the dog lover whose special dog is "just a pet." Helpful tips, how-tos, and features are written in an entertaining and reader-friendly format. It's a lifestyle magazine for today's busy families that want to enjoy the most rewarding, mutually happy relationship with their canine companions.

Dog Fancy

The world's most widely read dog magazine, *Dog Fancy* celebrates dogs and the people who love them. Each monthly issue includes info on cutting-edge medical developments, health and fitness (with a focus on prevention, treatment, and natural therapy), behavior and training, travel and activities, breed profiles and dog news, issues and trends for purebred and mixed breed dog owners. The magazine informs, inspires, and entertains readers while promoting responsible dog ownership. Throughout its more than forty-year history, *Dog Fancy* has garnered numerous honors, including being named the Best All-Breed Magazine by the Dog Writers Association of America.

Dog World

With more than ninety-five years of tradition as the top magazine for active people with active dogs, *Dog World* provides authoritative, valuable, and entertaining content to the community of

serious dog enthusiasts and participants, including breeders; conformation exhibitors; obedience, agility, herding, and field trial competitors; veterinarians; groomers; and trainers. This monthly magazine is the resource to turn to for up-to-date information about canine health, advanced training, holistic and homeopathic methods, breeding, and conformation and performance sports.

Dogs in Review

For more than fifteen years, *Dogs in Review* has showcased the finest dogs in the U.S. and from around the world. The emphasis has always been on strong editorial content, with input from distinguished breeders, judges, and handlers worldwide. This global perspective distinguishes this monthly publication from its competitors—no other North American dog-show magazine gathers together so many international experts to enlighten and entertain its readership.

Dogs USA

Dogs USA is an annual lifestyle magazine published by the editors of *Dog Fancy* that covers all aspects of the dog world: culture, art, history, travel, sports, and science. It also profiles breeds to help prospective owners choose the best dogs for their future needs, such as a potential show champion, super service dog, great pet, or competitive star.

Natural Dog

Natural Dog is the annual magazine dedicated to giving a dog a natural lifestyle. From nutritional choices to grooming to dog-supply options, this publication helps readers make the transition from traditional

to natural methods. The magazine also explores the array of complementary treatments available for today's dogs: acupuncture, massage, homeopathy, aromatherapy, and much more. *Natural Dog* appears as an annual publication and also as the flip side of *Dog Fancy* magazine four times a year (in February, May, August, and November).

Puppies USA

Also from the editors of *Dog Fancy,* this annual magazine offers essential information for all new puppy owners. *Puppies USA* is lively and informative, including advice on general care, nutrition, grooming and training techniques for all puppies, whether purebred or mixed breed, adopted, rescued, or purchased. In addition, it offers family fun through quizzes, contests, and much more. An extensive breeder directory is included.

WEBSITES

www.akc.org

The American Kennel Club's (AKC's) website is an excellent starting point for researching dog breeds and learning about puppy care. The site lists hundreds of breeders, along with basic information about breed selection and basic care. The site also has links to the national breed club of every AKC-recognized breed; breed-club sites offer plenty of detailed breed information, as well as lists of member breeders. In addition, you can find the AKC National Breed Club Rescue Network at www.akc.org/breeds/rescue.cfm. If looking for purebred puppies, go to www.puppybuyerinfo.com for AKC classifieds and parent club referrals.

www.dogchannel.com

Dog Channel is "the website for dog lovers," where hundreds of thousands of visitors each month find extensive information on breeds, training, health and nutrition, puppies, care, activities, and more. Interactive features include forums, Dog College, games, puzzles, and Club Dog, an exclusive free club where dog lovers can create blogs for their pets and earn points to buy products. DogChannel is the definitive one-stop site for all things dog.

www.meetthebreeds.com

The official website of the AKC Meet the Breeds® event, hosted by the American Kennel Club in the Jacob Javits Center in New York City in the fall. The first Meet the Breeds event took place in 2009. The website includes information on every recognized breed of dog and cat, alphabetically listed, as well as the breeders, demonstration facilitators, sponsors, and vendors participating in the annual event.

AKC AFFILIATES

The AKC Museum of the Dog, established in 1981, is located in St. Louis, Missouri, and houses the world's finest collection of art devoted to the dog.

The **AKC Humane Fund** promotes the joy and value of responsible and productive pet ownership through education, outreach, and grant-making. Monies raised may fund grants to organizations that teach responsible pet ownership; provide for the health and well-being of all dogs; and preserve and celebrate the human-animal bond and the evolutionary relationship between dogs and humankind.

The **American Kennel Club Companion Animal Recovery (CAR) Corporation** is dedicated to reuniting lost microchipped and tattooed pets with their owners. AKC CAR maintains a permanent-identification database and provides lifetime recovery services 24 hours a day, 365 days a year, for all animal species. Millions of pets are enrolled in the program. Coordinators have recovered hundreds of thousands of pets since the program's inception in 1995.

The American Kennel Club Canine Health Foundation (AKC CHF), Inc. is the largest foundation in the world to fund canine-only health studies for purebred and mixed-breed dogs. More than $22 million has been allocated in health-research funds to more than 500 studies conducted to help dogs live longer, healthier lives. Go to www.akcchf.org.

AKC PROGRAMS

The Canine Good Citizen® Program (CGC) was established in 1989 and is designed to recognize dogs that have good manners at home and in the community. This rapidly growing, nationally recognized program stresses responsible dog ownership for owners and basic training and good manners for dogs. All dog that pass the ten-step Canine Good Citizen® test receive a certificate from the American Kennel Club.

The **AKC S.T.A.R. Puppy Program** is designed to get dog owners and their puppies off to a good start and is aimed at loving dog owners who have taken the time to attend basic obedience classes with their puppies. After completing a six-week training course, the puppy must pass the AKC S.T.A.R. Puppy test, which evaluates Socialization, Training, Activity, and Responsibility.

The **AKC Therapy Dog** program recognizes all American Kennel Club dogs and their owners who have given their time and helped people by volunteering as a therapy dog and owner team. The AKC Therapy Dog program is an official AKC title awarded to dogs that have worked to improve the lives of the people they have visited. The AKC Therapy Dog title (AKC ThD) can be earned by dogs who have been certified by recognized therapy dog organizations. Visit www.akc.org/akctherapydog for more information.

Index

AMERICAN KENNEL CLUB®

Advocating for the purebred dog as a family companion, advancing canine health and well-being, working to protect the rights of all dog owners and promoting responsible dog ownership, the **American Kennel Club:**

Sponsors more than **22,000 sanctioned events** annually including conformation, agility, obedience, rally, tracking, lure coursing, earthdog, herding, field trial, hunt test, and coonhound events

Features a **10-step Canine Good Citizen® program** that rewards dogs who have good manners at home and in the community

Has reunited more than **400,000** lost pets with their owners through the AKC Companion Animal Recovery - visit **www.akccar.org**

Created and supports the AKC Canine Health Foundation, which funds research projects using the more than **$22 million** the AKC has donated since 1995 - visit **www.akcchf.org**

Joins **animal lovers** through education, outreach and grant-making via the AKC Humane Fund - visit **www.akchumanefund.org**

We're more than champion dogs. We're the dog's champion.

www.akc.org